Project Management
Fundamentals

Prometheus Training Corporation

Prometheus Training Corporation develops organizational learning solutions that enhance bottom-line business performance and productivity. Their areas of concentration include business management, quality, project management, customer service, sales, and health/safety/ environmental training. Prometheus has developed training packages for a wide range of industrial, commercial, government, educational, and institutional clients.

PROJECT MANAGEMENT: FUNDAMENTALS

Course Number: 079160
Course Edition: 1.4
For software version: xxxx

ACKNOWLEDGEMENTS

Project Team

Curriculum Developer and Technical Writer: Helene Geiger/ Prometheus Training Corporation

Project Support

Managing Editor: Mark Onisk • **Acquisition Editor:** Jennifer L. Hennard • **Technical Editor:** Charles E. Koster

NOTICES

HELP US IMPROVE OUR COURSEWARE

Your comments are important to us. Please contact us at Element K Press LLC, 1-800-478-7788, 500 Canal View Boulevard, Rochester, NY 14623, Attention: Product Planning, or through our Web site at **http://support.elementkcourseware.com**.

PROJECT MANAGEMENT: FUNDAMENTALS

CONTENT OVERVIEW

CONTENTS

LESSON 1: THE PROJECT MANAGEMENT LIFE CYCLE

LESSON 2: SETTING UP FOR SUCCESS

LESSON 3: THE PROJECT TEAM

Lesson 4: Risk Management

Lesson 5: Project Plans

Lesson 6: The Project Schedule

Lesson 7: The Project Budget

Lesson 8: Project Tracking and Control

CONTENTS

ABOUT THIS COURSE

Project Management Fundamentals provides an overview of basic of project management. It provides the theory and core methodology you will need to manage projects or participate on project teams.

Course Prerequisites

To ensure your success, we recommend you first take the following Element K course or have equivalent knowledge:

- *None*

Course Objectives

When you're done working your way through this course, you'll be able to:

- Discuss the phases of the Project Management Life Cycle and a project manager's role in each phase.
- List and discuss basic project success criteria and common reasons for project failure.
- Discuss techniques for setting up a strong project team.
- List and discuss elements of a Risk Management Plan.
- Discuss techniques for planning and sequencing project activities, including the Work Breakdown Structure and the Network Logic Diagram.
- Identify the Critical Path for completing a project on schedule.
- List and discuss the cost elements that should be included in a project budget.
- Discuss techniques for controlling for deviation from budgets and schedules.
- Discuss key elements of project management communications and reporting tools.
- Discuss key activities of Project Close-out.

COURSE SETUP INFORMATION

Hardware and Software Requirements

To run this course, you will need:

- Overhead projector
- Whiteboard projection screen, markers
- Overhead of objectives
- Overhead of agenda
- Overhead cells
- Flip chart and markers

Class Requirements

In order for the class to run properly, perform the procedures described below.

1. Set up the overhead projector to project onto the white board. Use the white board and markers to work through group exercises such as Task 6B-1.

List of Additional Files

Printed with each lesson is a list of files students open to complete the tasks in that lesson. Many tasks also require additional files that students do not open, but are needed to support the file(s) students are working with. These supporting files are included with the student data files on the course CD-ROM or data disk. Do not delete these files.

HOW TO USE THIS BOOK

You can use this book as a learning guide, a review tool, and a reference.

As a Learning Guide

Each lesson covers one broad topic or set of related topics. Lessons are arranged in order of increasing proficiency with *Project Management Fundamentals;* skills you acquire in one lesson are used and developed in subsequent lessons. For this reason, you should work through the lessons in sequence.

We organized each lesson into explanatory topics and step-by-step activities. Topics provide the theory you need to master *Project Management Fundamentals,* activities allow you to apply this theory to practical hands-on examples.

Through the use of hands-on activities, illustrations that give you feedback at crucial steps, and supporting background information, this book provides you with the foundation and structure to learn *Project Management Fundamentals* quickly and easily.

As a Review Tool

Any method of instruction is only as effective as the time and effort you are willing to invest in it. For this reason, we encourage you to spend some time reviewing the book's more challenging topics and activities.

As a Reference

You can use the Concepts sections in this book as a first source for definitions of terms, background information on given topics, and summaries of procedures.

Icons Serve As Cues:

Throughout the book, you will find icons representing various kinds of information. These icons serve as an "at-a-glance" reminder of their associated text.

Topic:

Represents the beginning of a topic

Task:

Represents the beginning of a task

Student Note:

A margin note that highlights information for students

QuickTip:

A margin note that represents a tip, shortcut, or additional way to do something

Web Tip:

A margin note that refers you to a website where you might find additional information

Overhead:

In the instructor edition, an overhead note refers to a .ppt slide that the instructor can use in the lesson

Instructor Note:

A margin note in the Instructor's Edition that gives tips for teaching the class

Check Your Skills:

Represents a Check Your Skills practice

Apply Your Knowledge:

Represents an Apply Your Knowledge activity

Glossary Term:

A margin note that represents a definition. This definition also appears in the glossary

Warning:

A margin note that represents a caution; this note typically provides a solution to a potential problem

Version Note:

A margin note that represents an alternate way to do something using a different version of the software

Additional Instructor Note:

A margin note in the instructor's Edition that refers the instructor to more information in the back of the book

The Project Management Life Cycle

Data Files
L1Wksht.doc

Lesson Time
30-40 minutes

Overview

Project management is one of today's most vital skills. Read any business journal's list of "Hot Careers" and you'll find project management at or near the top. Project management is a rewarding discipline, but also a demanding one. In this lesson, you will look at the "big picture" of what a project manager does over the course of a project.

Objectives

To discuss the phases in the Project Life Cycle and a project manager's role in each phase, you will:

1A   Differentiate between projects and non-projects, and explain how that difference impacts project management.

Managing projects is different from managing everyday tasks. Before you learn to manage projects, you need to know the difference between a project and ongoing work, and how that affects management activities.

1B   List the phases and deliverables for each phase in a project.

Every project is different, but they all progress through certain predictable phases. You will need to know what the phases in the project are, what activities occur in each phase, and what you will be expected to deliver at the end of each phase.

1C   Identify the roles of a project manager and list skills associated with each role.

Over the life of a project, the project manager must perform many duties. You will need to know what roles you might be expected to play.

Topic 1A

What is a Project?

Managing *projects* is different from managing everyday tasks. Before you learn to manage projects, be sure you know the difference between a project and ongoing work. The table below lists some of the differences.

Ongoing Work	Project Work
Repeating process	One of a kind, temporary process
No clear beginning or ending	Clear beginning and ending
Same output created each time the work is performed	Output is created only once
Everyone in work group performs similar functions	Requires multi-disciplined team

What is Project Management?

Project Management is the planning, organizing, scheduling, leading, communicating, and controlling of work activities to achieve a pre-defined outcome on time and within budget.

Project:
Work that has a specified beginning and ending and that produces a unique output.

Project management:
The planning, organizing, staffing, scheduling, leading, and controlling of work activities to achieve a pre-defined outcome on time and within budget.

PROGRESSIVELY
ELABORATION:
- NEW INFORMATION
THAT CAUSES CHANGES

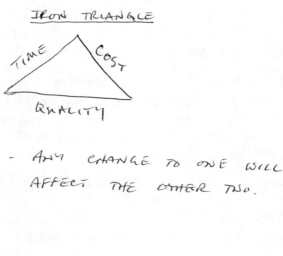

IRON TRIANGLE

TIME COST

QUALITY

- ANY CHANGE TO ONE WILL AFFECT THE OTHER TWO.

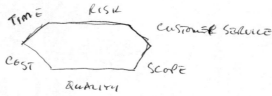

TIME   RISK   CUSTOMER SERVICE

COST   SCOPE

QUALITY

What Makes Project Management Different?

That is why project managers need to use special management tools to help control the risk. As you will learn, controlling risk is an important part of project management. Why is project management different from regular management? If you manage ongoing work, you can use experience to predict how much time, money, and equipment are needed to do a task. Unless something in the work process changes, your prediction is likely to be accurate.

If you are project manager, you can't rely solely on previous experience because each project is inherently unique. That makes managing projects riskier than managing ongoing work—there are no absolute rules for predicting how much time, money, and equipment you will need to complete the project successfully.

TASK 1A-1

Differentiating Between Projects and Non-Projects

1. **Bob manages a group of tax return processors. Every day, his people interview clients, use the data to fill out tax returns, and compute the amount of tax owed. Is Bob's group assigned to a project or ongoing work? Why?**

Rita's team is developing a training manual to help new Tax Return Processors learn their jobs faster. Her team is made up of Tax Return Specialists, writers, and graphic designers who are assigned to the team part-time. Rita's work began when her manager gave her the assignment, and must be completed by January 1 in time for Human Resources to train the new Tax Return Processors who will be hired next year. Is Rita's team assigned to a project or ongoing work?

Who has the more difficult management job—Rita or Bob? Why?

PROS MGR
RESPONSIBILITIES
1) IDENTIFY REQ'TS
FOR THE PROJ
2) ESTABLISH ACTION-
ABLE OBJECTIVES
3) BALANCE SCOPE,
TIME, & COST
- COMPARE TO
BASELINE
4) SATISFY EVERYONE'S
NEEDS - COMMUNICATE
TO ALL INVOLVED.

There is always an element of risk in any project. One of the goals of a project manager is to minimize or mitigate risk.

Topic 1B

The Project Management Life Cycle

Every project is unique, but they all progress through the same phases.

- Project Initiation
- Project Planning
- Project Implementation
- Project Close-Out

Figure 1-1 shows the project management activities in each phase.

The names and even the number of project phases may change from one organization to the next, but the same activities should take place in every project.

Some organizations break this Phase out into Concept and Feasibility phases.

Some organizations break this Phase out into Execution and Control phases.

PROJECT MANAGEMENT PHASES

PHASES

DELIVERABLES

INITIATION

Defining and Scoping

Identifying Stakeholders

Team Building

Making the Rules

> Project Charter
>
> Stakeholder Responsibility Matrix
>
> Statement of Work
>
> Team Charter

PLANNING

Budgeting

Scheduling

Activity Planning

> Deliverables Breakdown Structure
>
> Work Breakdown Structure
>
> Detailed Responsibility Matrix
>
> Schedule
>
> Budget
>
> Activity Plan

IMPLEMENTATION

Working the Plan

Monitoring Progress

Taking Corrective Action

Reporting Progress

> Status/Progress Reports
>
> Earned Value Analysis
>
> Change Requests

CLOSE-OUT

Handing Off to End Users

Closing Down Operations

Reporting Outcomes

> Final Report
>
> Personnel Evaluations

Figure 1-1: *Project phases, activities, and deliverables.*

Project Management Deliverables

In each phase, you create project management *deliverables* as an output of project management activities. You can review the most common deliverables in Figure 1-1. The names of these deliverables may be unfamiliar to you now, but you will work through them as you progress through the course. Right now, the important thing to know is that the deliverables from one project phase are used as tools to manage the next project phases. Also, don't get confused between these *project*

Handwritten margin notes:

PROJ. MGT. PROCESSES

STAKEHOLDER: VESTED BUSSINESS INTEREST IN THE SUCCESS OR FAILURE OF THE PROJECT.

EXECUTING

- BUSSINESS CASE: WHAT YOUR COMPANY WANTS OUT OF THIS PROJECT.
- RESTRAINT:
- ASSUMPTION:
- ENTERPRISE ENVIRONMENTAL FACTORS
- ORGANIZATIONAL PROCESS ASSETS

Deliverable:
An output from a project management activity. Deliverables from each phase are used to manage the next phases of the project.

management deliverables and any *product deliverables* (for example, an interim version of software) that might be created during a project.

Project Milestones

The end of each phase is often referred to as a *Project Milestone*. In some organizations, these are referred to as *Project Gates*. This is the time for the *stakeholders* in a project to evaluate the project's progress, suggest changes, and decide whether to continue or discontinue working on the project.

Progression of Risk

Project risk is managed most cost-effectively in the early project phases. As illustrated in the following figure, stakeholders can still change direction or fine-tune their plans in the early phases without realizing large losses from sunk costs. That is why good project managers build in risk management planning activities as early as possible in the project. As a rule, projects in which risk is well-managed in the early phases have a greater probability of meeting their planned time, budget, and quality goals.

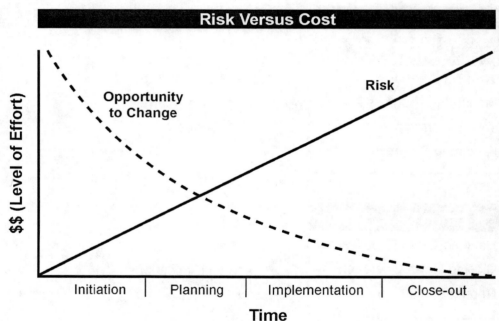

Project Milestone:
The end point of a project phase; a formal review time at which stakeholders make a go/no-go decision about continuing the project. Also known as Project Gate.

Project Gate:
The end point of a project phase; a formal review time at which stakeholders make a go/no-go decision about continuing the project. Also known as Project Milestone.

Stakeholder:
Someone who has a business interest in the outcome of the project. Although most stakeholders are project team members, they are not required to be. For example, senior managers or customers may be key stakeholders, but do not personally participate in project work.

TASK 1B-1

Discussing Project Steps and Deliverables

1. In which project phase will the project's stakeholders set goals for the project?

2. In which project phase will the scheduling and budgeting be done?

3. In which project phase does the project manager need to monitor whether work is progressing according to schedule and budget predictions?

4. In which phase does the greatest expense typically occur? Why?

Topic 1C

The Role of the Project Manager

Project managers play a variety of roles over the life of a project. Here are some of the roles that a project manager plays, as well as the skills needed for each role.

Role	Skills Needed
• Leader	• Leadership
• Planner	• Team building
• Organizer	• Management
• Controller	• Time management
• Communicator	• Delegation
• Negotiator	• Estimating and budgeting
• Peace maker	• Risk management
• Advocate	• Software proficiency *-MICROSOFT -PRIMAVERA*
• Risk manager	• Scheduling
	• Interviewing
	• Questioning
	• Persuading
	• Team facilitation
	• Conflict resolution
	• Negotiation
	• Writing
	• Presentation
	• Upwards, downwards, and sideways communication
	• Technical skills
	• Political savvy

To succeed in project management, you will need the traditional management skills—planning, organizing and controlling—but you will need to adapt them for a project setting. You will need excellent communication skills, both oral and written. Finally, you will need superior people skills: leadership, motivation, team building, consensus building, conflict resolution and negotiation skills.

One last thing. As a project manager, you will need to tolerate ambiguity. Remember, your project has never been done before. It is up to you to decide how your team will reach its goal.

TASK 1C-1

Discussing the Project Manager's Role

Objective:

Setup: Frank Edwardson has just been handed a plum assignment – managing the development of Standard Publishing's first cookbook. The project is a high-profile one. Standard has hired the famous but volatile TV Chef, Francesca Tosca, to create the recipes. As a result, Marketing reports that there is already a lot of media buzz around the project.

1. **Standard chose Frank Edwards as project manager because they knew he had excellent communications skills. In what phases of the Italian Cookbook project will Frank need to use these skills? Will the communications be upwards, downwards, or sideways?**

UPWARD – MGT

ONWARD – TEAM MEMBERS

SIDEWAYS – OTHER DEPT

Summary

In this lesson, you learned how projects are different from non-projects, and why special project management skills are needed to lead projects. You were introduced to the phases of a typical project, the steps in each phase, and deliverables for each phase. Finally, you discussed the many roles that a project manager must play over the course of a project.

Apply Your Knowledge 1-1

Suggested Time:
10 minutes

Project Management Portfolio: Skills Evaluation and Action Planning

Objective: Evaluate your project management skill set and decide what areas need improvement.

Instructions: Over the course of this program, you will receive a portfolio of tools that you can use in your own projects. This is the first sheet in the Portfolio. Take a few minutes to fill it in now. You will find a blank version of this worksheet on the CD-ROM that accompanies this book. You may wish to use the blank version of this worksheet with other members of your team.

Project Management Portfolio: Skills Evaluation and Action Planning

1. What is the name of your project?
2. What is your role on the project?
3. Rate your current skill levels below (H = High, M = Medium, L = Low
4. Rate your required skill level (the level that is required for your role on this project)
5. Rate the priority for this skill level (how important is the skill for this project)
6. List any action that should be taken to improve your skills. (Actions might include training, working with a mentor or coach, seeking a developmental assignment, reading books or articles, etc.)
7. You may wish to share your findings with your manager or team leader.

Skill	Current Skill Level (H,M,L)	Required Skill Level (H,M,L)	Priority (H,M,L)	Recommended Action
Technical Skills				
Management Skills (Planning, Organizing, Controlling, etc.)				
Software Proficiency (Project Management Software)				
Estimating and Budgeting skills				
Risk Management skills				
Leadership & Motivation Skills				
Delegation Skills				
Communication skills (questioning, persuading, presenting, writing)				
Team Building skills (consensus building, conflict resolution, team decision-making)				
Team Facilitation skills				
Negotiation Skills				

Lesson Review

1A Which items below are characteristics of a project?

____ a. Only one person at a time is working on the task.

____ b. The task has a clear beginning and ending.

____ c. The task results in the same output each time it is performed.

____ d. The resources required to perform the task are known based on previous experience.

1B The project phase in which budgets are created is commonly called the:

____ a. Initiation Phase.

____ b. Planning Phase.

____ c. Implementation Phase.

____ d. Close-Out Phase.

1C List four skills needed by a project manager.

Setting Up for Success

LESSON 2

Data Files
L2Repts.doc
L2SOW.doc
L2Stkhldrs.doc

Lesson Time
30-40 minutes

Overview

"If I had an hour to save the world, I would spend 50 minutes defining the problem and 10 minutes executing the solution." — *Albert Einstein*

In order for your project to succeed, you must lay a firm foundation during the Initiation Phase of the project management life cycle. This is the time to define what the project will accomplish, identify project stakeholders, and establish clear, agreed-upon success criteria for your project. The major deliverables from the Initiation Phase are the Stakeholder Responsibility Matrix, Project Charter, and Statement of Work.

Objectives

To identify the activities and deliverables generated in the Initiation Phase of a project, you will:

2A   Discuss project success criteria and common reasons for project failures.

What makes a project succeed or fail? These guidelines will help you get your project on track and keep it there.

2B   List and identify activities and deliverables generated in the Initiation Phase.

Activities during the Initiation Phase focus on identifying roles and responsibilities, defining project goals, and setting up rules for how the project will run. The output of these activities is documented in the Statement of Work, Project Charter, and Stakeholder Responsibility Matrix.

2C   List and identify elements needed to define a project's purpose, scope and success criteria.

What will your project try to accomplish? What won't it try to accomplish? This section explains what you'll need to clearly define your project.

2D   List and identify the required and optional elements of a Statement of Work.

The Statement of Work is a major deliverable of the Initiation Phase. Adapt it to fit its intended audience and the way it will be used.

2E   Discuss the purpose and elements of the Project Charter.

The Project Charter provides official authorization for project activities and expenditures.

Topic 2A

The Meaning of Success

The Three Constraining Factors

Projects don't happen in vacuums. If someone is willing to pay you to manage a project, you can be sure there is a strategic reason for the project to exist. Someone needs the project output by a particular date. They have a limited amount of money to pay for the project output. And they need the project output to be fit for a particular purpose.

These three factors—time, cost, and quality—constrain every project. They are interrelated and exist in a state of equilibrium. Change any one factor, and the other two will be affected as well.

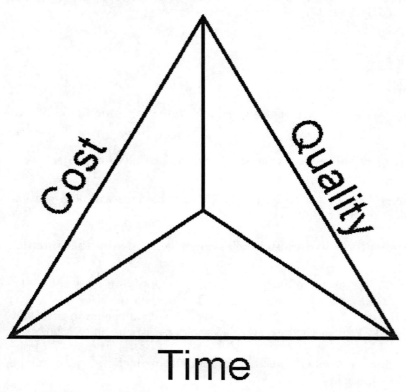

Figure 2-1: *The three success factors.*

How Do You Define Success?

The basic criteria for success on *every* project are:

- On time
- Within budget
- High quality (satisfying or exceeding customer quality expectations)

So what does success mean for *your* project? During the *Initiation Phase* , your job is to help stakeholders spell out exactly what they mean by on time, within budget, and high quality. You will need good people skills as you negotiate trade-offs among these factors, to arrive at a definition of success that is achievable. And you will need your communication skills to make sure that you, the stakeholders, and your team all share a common understanding of the meaning of success.

Common Project Problems

Here is a list of typical project problems:

- Dissatisfied customers or stakeholders
- Misunderstood deliverables
- Inappropriate budgets
- Inappropriate schedules
- Overworked or underworked resources

What do these problems have in common? They all stem from poorly understood success criteria—criteria that should have been established and shared in the Initiation Phase. And they all show up in later phases, when the cost of corrective action is high.

A Word of Warning

In an ideal world, project managers work on a project from the start of the Initiation Phase. In the real world, you may join your project later. As Project Manager, it is up to you to insist that the proper foundation is laid during the Initiation Phase. If you are handed a project that is already underway, backtrack and work with the stakeholders to define clear success criteria before moving forward.

Initiation Phase:
The project phase in which project mission, goals, and scope are defined. The output of the Initiation Phase is a Statement of Work.

As Project Manager, it is up to you to insist that the proper foundation is laid during the Initiation Phase.

TASK 2A-1

What's Wrong Here?

Setup: Jennifer has just been assigned to manage the retooling of a manufacturing line. Her Vice-President of Manufacturing wants the work completed in 6 months, and will authorize payment of up to $500,000.

1. **What success criterion is missing?**

   QUALITY / SCOPE

2. **If you were Jennifer, what questions would you want answered?**

   - DEFINE RETOOLING
   - DEFINE QUALITY/SCOPE
   - WHO
   - STAKEHOLDERS ?

Topic 2B

What Happens in the Initiation Phase?

Activities and Deliverables

Activities during the Initiation Phase focus on identifying stakeholders, ascertaining their roles and responsibilities, defining project success criteria, and setting up ground rules for the project. Figure 2-2 shows major activities, as well as the deliverables that are created as outputs from the Initiation Phase.

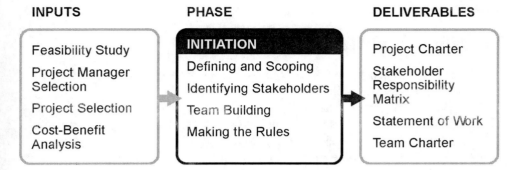

Figure 2-2: *Initiation phase of the project management life cycle.*

Notice that there are "inputs" to the Initiation Phase (see Figure 2–2). Organizations may use a variety of criteria for selecting a project. Sometimes, the selection and justification for a project are conducted at the executive level. Other projects are approved at the manager level. Whether they have been carried out formally or informally, by executive level staff or otherwise, this information is important input into the definition and criteria-setting activities for the project.

Most of the Deliverables from the Initiation Phase (see Figure 2–2) will be explained later in this lesson. The exception is the Team Charter, which will be discussed in Lesson 3.

FEASIBILITY: CAN IT BE DONE W/ CURRENT CONSTRAINTS.

COST-BENEFIT ANALYSIS: COST VS EFFORT

Some organizations consider the Feasibility Study and other "inputs" to be part of the Initiation Phase rather than precursors to it.

TASK 2B-1

Discussing Activities and Deliverables

Setup: When he received his assignment, Frank Edwardson asked to see all available documentation on the Italian Cookbook project. He hoped to see a list of potential projects, each with their strategic goals and expected costs and benefits itemized. He also expected to see a feasibility study for the cookbook line—a new product line for the company. Shockingly, the only documentation available was written on the back of a dinner napkin. The napkin said, "sell 10,000 books @ $79; assumes development >$125,000, production <$10 per book."

1. **Does the napkin constitute a cost/benefit analysis? How useful are the figures provided on the napkin?**

   - No
   - Figures are not traceable
   - How old are the figures

2. **What should the project manager do if inputs such as a feasibility study or cost/benefit analysis are not available for the project?**

   Go back to stakeholders asking or reviewing the feasibility or cost/benefit analysis.

Topic 2C

Project Definition and Scope

How Do You Define a Project?

As you've already learned, you define the project during the Initiation Phase. But what goes into a project definition? In one form or another, the "definition" should include these elements:

- Stakeholders and their responsibilities
- Project purpose
- Project objectives
- Project scope
- Project sign-off and review hierarchies
- Project reporting and communications plan

Project Stakeholders

Stakeholders are people with a business interest in your project. Here is a list of stakeholders on a typical project:

Sponsor	• Has authority over the project.
	• Signs off on all planning documents and change requests.
	• Provides team with resources.
	• Champions and mentors the team and project manager.
	• Reviews progress and quality.
	• Cuts through red tape and expedites activities.
	• Signs and publishes the project charter.
Customers	• Takes delivery of the project output.
	• Pays for the project output.
	• Provides specifications for project output.
	• May be multiple individuals or companies, with conflicting requirements and specifications.
Functional Managers	• Impacted by project activities or project outcome.
	• Contribute resources to project (people, equipment, etc.).
	• May have conflicting requirements for project outcome.
	• Project manager's manager may be included.

Project Manager	• Works with stakeholders to define the project.
	• Plans, schedules, and budgets project activities.
	• Works with team to carry out plans.
	• Monitors performance and takes corrective action.
	• Keeps sponsor and stakeholders informed.
	• Requests and documents scope changes.
	• Acts as liaison between stakeholders and project team.
Project Team Members	• Assigned based on ability to handle specific project activities.
	• May include internal and external resources.
	• Interface with sponsor and other stakeholders through project manager.

Stakeholders have conflicting needs and priorities. It is important to get them involved during the Initiation Phase, so they can participate in reaching consensus agreement on what constitutes "success" for the project.

TASK 2C-1

Identifying Stakeholders

> **Setup:** Refer to the Stakeholder Responsibility Matrix for the Italian Cookbook scenario.

1. **Review the Stakeholder Responsibility Matrix for the Italian Cookbook scenario.**

   This is a way to document stakeholder roles and responsibilities. Stakeholders must sign off on this document during the Initiation Phase.

2. **Suppose that the project is in the Implementation Phase when Frank Edwardson learns that the Facilities Manager is refusing to make available the kitchen facilities that Frank was counting on. How can Frank use the Stakeholder Responsibility Matrix to help get what he needs?**

By signing off on the Stakeholder Responsibility Matrix, stakeholders commit to fulfilling their obligations later in the project.

3. **Frank has noticed that no customers were included on the stakeholder team! What should you do if you join a project late, and realize that a key stakeholder has been left out of the project definition activities?**

Project Purpose

Every project needs a Purpose Statement to lay out why the project exists and what it is supposed to achieve. The Purpose Statement includes two elements:

- *NEED* → Problem Statement – Determines what problem will the project solve or what opportunity will the project exploit?

- *HOW* → Mission Statement – Determines what approach will be taken, for whom, and by when.

It may take a while to get all the stakeholders to agree on the Purpose Statement. Take the time to do it right. This statement is the foundation for all other project activities. Once written, refer to it often as you make decisions in later project phases.

In some projects, the Mission Statement and Problem Statement are separate documents.

TASK 2C-2

Identifying Elements of the Purpose Statement

Setup: Standard Publishing's Italian Cookbook will be the first in a line of celebrity-chef cookbooks. Standard, a longtime leader in health-related self-help publishing, has seen a fall-off in market share as consumers turn to the Internet for free health information. Standard wants the cookbooks to help leverage their health-conscious image, appeal to a new customer base of upscale food-lovers, and provide information that is impractical to publish on the Internet. Standard wants to introduce their new cookbook line in October, to coordinate with Francesca Tosca's new TV season. That means the books have to be available at booksellers by August 31.

1. **What problem does the project solve?**

   FALLOFF IN MKT SHARE

2. **What approach will be taken, for whom, and by when?**

   UP SCALE, HEALTH CONSCIOUS CELEBRATIES

3. **During the Implementation Phase of the project, Frank Edwardson's team decides to develop a software program to automate the conversion between American and Italian measurement units. How can the Purpose Statement guide Frank and his team in deciding whether this activity is a good idea?**

   - ASK PERTINANT QUESTIONS TO AVOID SCOPE CREEP.

   - ADDITIONAL PHASES

Project Goals and Objectives

Taken together, *project goals and objectives* are the target your project needs to hit. They spell out how you intend to accomplish your project purpose, and what success criteria you intend to meet.

Articulating project goals and objectives help stakeholders come to a common understanding of what the project's outcome will look like, as well as what it will take to achieve it. They should include enough detail so everyone understands:

- What you intend to do to achieve the project purpose
- Results you intend to produce
- What performance levels will be considered acceptable for each result

Performance levels are the time, cost, and quality goals that apply to your project. They should be stated in a way that is measurable.

Here is a set of project goals and objectives for a retooling project:

Project Goals and Objectives

1. Replace the current cutting and soldering machines with computerized machines by September 1, 2001. Replacement changeover must take place within a maximum of 2 weeks.
2. Select a computerized cutting machine that can interface with our current manufacturing equipment and that can cut to tolerances of .0005mm or lower.
3. Retrain operators on new equipment by September 5, 2001.
4. Total cost of project not to exceed $1.5 million.

Stakeholders need to evaluate a project's goals and objectives carefully. Some questions that stakeholders should ask include:

- Are the goals and objectives <u>aligned with</u> the organization's <u>strategic goals</u>?
- Are the goals and objectives <u>realistic</u>?
- Can the organization <u>afford</u> to meet the goals and objectives (does it have the time/money/expertise to do the job)?
- Are there <u>additional success criteria</u> that should be included?

The project manager's job is to accomplish the goals and objectives successfully. If you feel that the goals and objectives for your project are unclear or incomplete, work with your stakeholders to create a statement that gives you the direction you need to hit your target.

TASK 2C-3

Examining Project Goals and Objectives

Setup: In the Italian Cookbook scenario, Frank and the stakeholders have determined that they need to complete the book development by July 31. After that, it will be turned over to Production and Marketing, who need to get it out the door by August 31. The upper limit for development cost is $200,000. Mme. Tosca's compensation, which includes an advance payment and royalties, is not included in that amount. Development is defined as creating the recipes, testing them, photographing them, working with Mme. Tosca to create interesting anecdotal information about the recipes, adding additional writing and graphics, and combining all of this into book form. The book must have at least 100 recipes, at least 20 attractive full-page color photos, lots of white space for making notes, and a picture of Mme. Tosca on the cover. It cannot be more than 200 pages long.

1. **What tasks does the project manager have to accomplish in the project? What output should result? What performance levels must be met?**

   7/31   < 200 k

   LAYOUT WORK
   - 100 RECIPES
   - 20 PHOTOS
   - 200 PAGES
   - ANECDOTEL INFO

Project Scope

How big should your project be? A *project scope* statement explains what is included—and what is not included—in your project. This is where you document any assumptions or constraints that may limit what your project can accomplish.

Use your Project Scope statement to avoid *scope creep*. This is additional work that attaches itself to your project, and that will keep you from hitting your time, cost, or quality goals.

project scope:
What is and is not included in your project.

scope creep:
Additional task items that are added to the project and that make it difficult to achieve project goals.

TASK 2C-4

Examining Project Scope

Setup: The scope statement for the Italian Cookbook scenario is, "Create an Italian Cookbook based on Mme. Tosca's favorite Southern Italian recipes that are suitable to be served at dinner. This includes appetizers, main dishes, pastas, and desserts."

1. Which of these is out of scope for the Italian Cookbook project?

SCOPE CREEP

✓ a. A recipe for Fettucine Alfredo, Mme. Tosca's favorite <u>Northern</u> Italian pasta. *Southern*

✓ b. The traditional <u>breakfast</u> food of Southern Italy. *dinner*

____ c. Recipes for Southern Italian dishes that Mme. Tosca served at dinner parties she catered in the White House.

Sign-Off and Review

As you progress through your project, you will produce interim deliverables. Some of them are *project management deliverables*, such as a Project Plan or Progress Report. There will also be interim *product deliverables*, such as:

- A first-draft of the Italian Cookbook

- An individual lesson in the new-hire training manual

- An equipment purchase recommendation in the retooling scenario

In the Initiation Phase, specify which deliverables require stakeholder review and sign-off before further work can proceed. Be sure to specify which stakeholders must be included in the sign-off.

Reporting Plan

It's important to keep stakeholders informed of project progress. But too much information can be overwhelming. In the Initiation Phase, create a Reporting Plan that will provide stakeholders with what they need to know, when they need to know it. The plan should explain:

- When to report   *• WHAT FORMAT ?*

- Which stakeholders should receive each report

- What to include in each report

- Where archival copies of reports can be found

You will learn more about the elements of a communications and reporting plan in Lesson 9.

Some organizations refer to this plan as a Communications Plan.

Topic 2D

Putting Together a Statement of Work

The Statement of Work

The *Statement of Work* (*SOW*) describes the work that will be performed in the project. Some organizations have a required format for their SOWs. Others leave it up to the Project Manager or author.

At minimum, include all the project definition elements in a SOW:

- Stakeholder Responsibility Matrix
- Project purpose
- Project objectives
- Project scope
- Sign-off and review hierarchy
- Communications and reporting plan

Add additional elements depending on your audience and how the SOW will be used. For example, for an audience of internal stakeholders only, you might add:

- A feasibility study.
- A cost-benefit analysis.
- Narrative descriptions of each project task.
- Assumptions or constraints.

On the other hand, if the SOW will be used as a specification document for outside suppliers, you probably should include:

- Milestone lists and delivery schedules.
- Precise specifications for each deliverable and milestone.
- Work Breakdown Structure (see Lesson 4).

The SOW can get long. It's a good idea to create a Summary Page or Contents Page to help readers find the important information quickly.

Statement of Work:
Describes the work that will be performed in the project.

SOW:
Statement of Work. It describes the work that will be performed in the project.

TASK 2D-1

Discussing the Statement of Work

1. **What should you do if you are asked to manage a project after the SOW is complete?**

2. **What should you do if your company does not normally use a SOW in its projects, although the company does required all of the elements listed above?**

Topic 2E

The Project Charter

The Project Charter

The Project Charter is an official statement that the project is backed by—and funded by—the organization. Usually, the Project Charter is signed and published by the project's sponsor.

Don't expect to see the Project Charter published on a parchment scroll, or even in an inch-thick binder. The Project Charter may be a short memo or a multi-page document, but should contain:

*   Name, purpose, and objectives of project.
*   Name of project manager.
*   Authorization for using organizational resources.

TASK 2E-1

Discussing the Project Charter

1. As project manager, Frank Edwardson will need to staff his project soon. How might he use the Project Charter for his staffing activities?

Summary

The Initiation Phase is the time to define what will happen in the project and how project success will be measured. One output of the Initiation Phase, the Project Charter, provides authorization for the project. Another output, the Stakeholder Responsibility Matrix, lists the roles and responsibilities of each project stakeholder. A third output is the Statement of Work. It should include, at minimum, these elements:

- Stakeholder list
- Project purpose
- Project objectives
- Project scope
- Sign-off and review hierarchy
- Reporting plan

Other elements of the SOW, including:

1. Milestone lists and delivery schedules
2. Precise specifications for each deliverable and milestone
3. A Work Breakdown Structure (see Lesson 4) may be added based on who will use the document and how it will be used.

Suggested Time:
10

Apply Your Knowledge 2-1

Project Portfolio: Statement of Work – Executive Summary

Objective: Use this worksheet to draft a preliminary Statement of Work for your project.

Instructions: Take a few moments to review this worksheet in your Project Portfolio. You will find a blank version on the CD-ROM that accompanies this book. The worksheet is meant to serve as a template. You can use it as an informal Executive Summary for your project's SOW. Or, use it as your personal checklist of required elements that must be attached to your SOW.

Lesson Review

2A **What are the three basic success criteria for every project?**

2B **Which of these are activities that occur during the Initiation Phase of a project?**

_____ a. Activity scheduling

_____ b. Conducting customer-satisfaction focus groups

_____ c. Defining time, cost, and quality criteria for the project

_____ d. All of the above are correct

2C **List six items that define a project and explain the expectations for its success.**

2D **Which of these elements should be included in a Statement of Work?**

_____ a. Objectives

_____ b. Supplier Contracts

_____ c. Stakeholder Roles and Responsibilities

_____ d. Project Budget

2E   What is the purpose of the Project Charter?

___   a. Provides official authorization for the project

___   b. States the project's success criteria

___   c. Lists all team members assigned to the project

___   d. Documents how the project team will report to stakeholders

The Project Team

Data Files
L3SkMtx.doc
L3Tmchrtr.doc
L3TmQus.doc

Lesson Time
30-40 minutes

Overview

"If I knew how to do everything myself, I would work alone." – Thomas Alva Edison

Projects tend to be too complex for one individual to carry out alone. You will need a multi-disciplined team to create your project output. Selecting the individual team members and developing them into a cohesive team unit is part of the art of project management.

Objectives

To discuss techniques used in setting up and running an effective project team, you will:

3A   Discuss techniques for setting up a strong project team.

What is a project team? How do you select individual team members and how do you mold them into a team? In this section, you'll get a chance to discuss some of the realities of working with organizational teams.

3B   Evaluate criteria for selecting team members.

Use task-related criteria to select core team members. The core team members will use similar criteria to select members of the implementation team.

3C   List and discuss the elements of a Team Charter

Teams work best when everyone knows what is expected of themselves and one another. The Team Charter documents the rules that the team will live by and sets standards for team member behavior.

PROJECT TEAM:
SKILLS
COMMITTED

CORE TEAM:

IMPLEMENTATION
TEAM:

Topic 3A

The Teamwork Challenge

What Makes Your Group a Team?

Look at any set of project objectives. Would you be able to carry out those objectives on your own? Most projects require a multi-disciplined team to perform the tasks required to accomplish the objectives. Building this team is one of the most difficult challenges for a project manager, and one of the most important.

A *project team* is more than a group of individuals who collectively have the skills required to do a project. On a team, the individuals must be committed to working together to reach a common goal. Getting from project group-hood to team-hood is a difficult process that starts with team member selection and continues through the life of the project.

project team:
Individuals who collectively possess the skills to do a project, and who are committed to working together to reach the project goals.

"It takes strong players to win a game. It takes a strong team to win a championship." – Michael Jordan

One of the complicating factors for project teams is that the team's membership may change over the course of a project. Figure 3–1 shows how team membership changes over a typical project management life cycle. During the Initiation Stage, a *core team* is selected. The core team helps the project manager plan for and select *Implementation Team* members who may be needed to carry out the Implementation and Close-Out phases of the project. Team membership grows during the Implementation phase. Some Implementation team members may stay with the team for short stretches of time, while others may stay throughout the entire Implementation Phase. During the Close-Out phase, only those team members who are responsible for hand-off activities remain on the Implementation Team. Throughout all of this activity, the project manager must keep the team unified and focused on its goal.

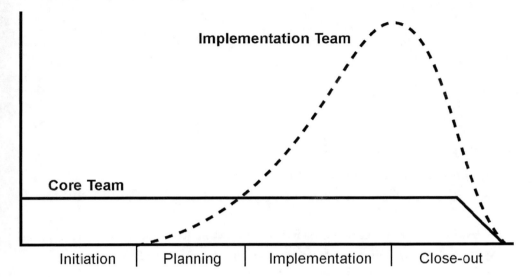

Figure 3-1: *Typical team membership during project management life cycle.*

2 **core team:**
Key individuals who represent the major activities that the team will undertake during the project.

3 **implementation team:**
Project team members who help to carry out activities planned by the Core Team.

Where Do Core Team Members Come From?

On some projects, the project manager picks the core team. However, in many projects, the core team is selected by the stakeholders. The project manager may be able to add individuals, but it is often politically difficult to remove individuals who were selected by the stakeholders.

Frequently, core team members report directly to other managers rather than to the project manager, as in Figure 3–2. Core team members will spend a large percentage of their time on the project, but may be expected to carry out other high-priority duties as well. The project manager may have to negotiate with other functional managers to free up more of the core team members' time to devote to the project.

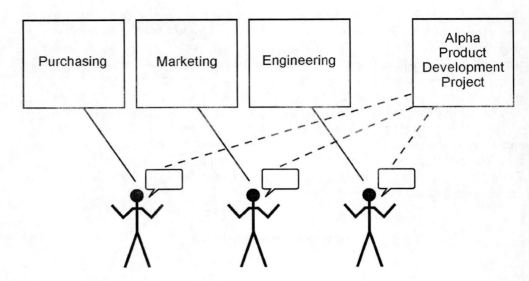

Figure 3-2: *Matrixed organization chart.*

Getting to Team-Hood

The keys to creating a strong project team include:

- Selecting individuals who have the required skills, attitudes, and time availability.
- Creating commitment to achieving the project goals.
- Helping team members to learn to trust one another and their cumulative abilities to achieve the project goals.

Figure 3–3 below shows the steps that a project manager must take to create an effective team.

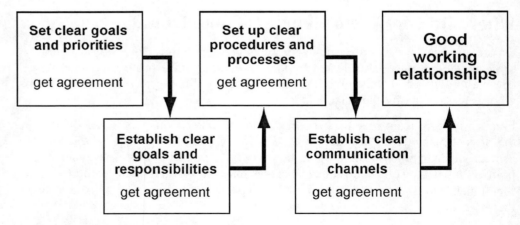

Figure 3-3: *Team building flow chart.*

Handwritten margin notes:

PROJ TYPES

1) FUNCTIONAL WORK:
   INTERDEPARTMENTAL
   WORK.

2) PROJECTIZED ORG:
   PROJ MGR HAS
   DECISION MAKING
   CAPABILITIES

3) COMPOSITE ORG
   CATCH ALL FOR
   OTHER TYPES

Getting good players is easy. Getting them to work together is the hard part. – Casey Stengel

It is rare to find individuals who have available time for a project. Typically, their availability must be negotiated with their management.

CLEAR + PRECISE COMMUNICATION

Topic 3B

Selecting Team Members

Task-Related Criteria

The project objectives specified a number of tasks that must be achieved over the course of the project. On a small project, core team members should be chosen based on their abilities to accomplish these tasks. On a larger or more complex project, core team members should be chosen based on their abilities to manage those who can accomplish these tasks.

Use a Skills Matrix like the one in Figure 3–4 to help you identify what skills you need for each task, and the level of skill required. You can use the completed Skills Matrix to help you select core team members, or to help you identify skills that your current team is missing. Later in the Planning phase, the core team can create a similar Skills Matrix to identify skills needed on the implementation team.

Team Skills Matrix

Selection Criteria

Skills	Skills Level Req'd for job	Supervision Req'd for job	Experience Level Req'd for job	Education Level Req'd for job	Team Member
Cooking	Main dishes, sauces Familiar with Italian ingredients Can convert from Italian to US metrics	Ability to work unsupervised but willing to work under direction of Mme Tosca Willing to work from recipes	Minimun 3 years as restaurant head chef; small restaurant experience desirable	Culinary School certificate desirable but not requ'd	Warren Scarpia
Baking	Italian-style pastry and cakes Familiar with Italian ingredients Can convert from Italian to US metrics	Ability to work unsupervised but willing to work under direction of Mme Tosca Willing to work from recipes	Minimum 3 years as pastry chef; small restaurant or bakery experience desirable	Culinary School certificate desirable but not req'd	Sandra Oldenberg
Assisting in kitchen (cooking)	Stirring Basting Making pasta Chopping vegetables Grinding meats Washing dishes	Supervised	Minimum 1 year professional kitchen experience		
Assisting in kitchen (baking)	Whipping Cream Chopping fruits Shaving chocolate Mixing pastry dough Washing pans	Supervised	Minimum 1 year professional kitchen experience (pastry concentration)		Carl Cavarradossi
Writing	Procedural (recipe) writing Interviewing Editing	Unsupervised	Minimum 5 years technical writing, at least 3 cookbook projects	B.A.	
Photography					
Graphic Design					
Page Layout					

Figure 3-4: *Skills matrix.*

TASK 3B-1

Using a Skills Matrix to Identify Needed Skills

Objective: Use a skills matrix to help you determine which skills are needed to accomplish each objective.

Setup: Refer to the Team Skills Matrix for the Italian Cookbook project.

- IDENTIFY SKILLS NEEDED OR SKILLS LACKING

1. For each project objective, brainstorm a list of skills required to accomplish the objective. Write the skills in the left column of the skills matrix.

2. For each skill, enter criteria you could use to measure whether someone has met the skill requirement. The criteria should include the amount of supervision required for the job, the amount or level of experience required, and the education level required.

3. After all skills and criteria have been identified, match them up against the credentials of your existing core team members, and write the names of the appropriate core team members in the corresponding box in the right-hand column.

4. Look for blank spaces in the right-hand column. These are indicators that your team lacks needed skills.

5. **If you were the project manager for the Italian Cookbook project, how might you respond to the blank spaces?**

Topic 3C

The Team Charter

Why a Team Charter Matters

Teams are just people working together. You'll be choosing the most skilled individuals you can find—people who may be experts at their jobs but may not know how to get things done in a group. You'll be working with these people to plan the project and make decisions, and there may be times when team members disagree with one another. You may have team members who want to arrive late for meetings, or who stay silent during decision making and then refuse to go along with the group's decision, or who don't seem to carry their own weight. How can you help the team be productive, focus on the project, and shake off all the interpersonal minutia that can distract them from their goal?

The Team Charter is a set of rules that the team creates to set a <u>standard of inter-personal behavior.</u> The rules vary based on need, but should include rules about:

- Meetings — TIME ; AGENDA
- Interpersonal Behavior
- Record Keeping — ACCOUNTIBILITY
- Decision Making
- Resources
- Communications

The Team Charter is a living document. It can and should change as the team's needs change. Spend time creating a charter with the core team and again with the implementation team and sub-teams. Review the Team Charter with the team or with individuals when interpersonal problems arise, or when the team wishes to change the team rules.

TASK 3C-1

Evaluating a Team Charter

Objective: Identify items that might be included on a Team Charter.

Setup: Refer to the Team Charter for the Italian Cookbook project. This document is included as a datafile on the CD-ROM.

1. **Can you think of an additional rule that might be included in the Meetings area?** WHEN? WHAT TIME?

2. **Why do you think it is important to include items like "avoid blaming other team members" or "avoid making negative comments about other team members' ideas" in the rules?**

3. **Mme. Tosca is an invaluable asset to the team, but sometimes she can ramble on and waste too much time in meetings. You don't want to keep her from talking, but you want to make sure that you cover necessary topics and that other people get their opinions heard, too. How might you write a rule to address the Mme. Tosca problem (without hurting Mme. Tosca's feelings!)?**

Summary

Most of the work on a project gets done by teams. Some of the most important tasks of project management include selecting team members, setting clear expectations and motivating team members to meet them, and helping teams to trust one another and their cumulative ability to succeed in the project.

The Team Skills Matrix is a useful tool to use in planning for project needs and selection of team personnel. It can be started at the core team level, then expanded to cover the implementation team. The team charter is a set of team behavior guidelines. Individual teams and sub-teams on the project may have their own team charters, and the team charters may evolve over the course of the project.

Apply Your Knowledge 3-1

Building a Team Charter

Suggested Time:
5-10 minutes

> **Objective:** Use the list of questions to create a Team Charter for your team.

Instructions: Take a few moments to review this worksheet in your Project Portfolio. (You will also find a blank copy on your CD-ROM.) Use the list of questions to help your team brainstorm rules that fit your project's needs. With your project team, brainstorm a list of rules, using the questions as a guideline.

Lesson Review

3A In which project phase should team building activities occur?

3B A Team Skills Matrix can be used to:

_____ a. Break out skills needed for each project task.

_____ b. Identify which team members have which skill sets.

_____ c. Identify criteria that may be used to determine whether a team member has a particular skill set.

_____ d. All of the above.

3C List six areas that should be addressed on the Project Charter.

Risk Management

Data Files
L4rsk.doc

Lesson Time
30-40 minutes

Overview

"The real risk is doing nothing." — Denis Waitley and Remi L. Witt in "Joy of Working," 1985.

Projects are inherently risky. Money, time, reputations, and sometimes even people's lives can be at stake in a project. While no one can completely eliminate risk, the discipline of project management has evolved strategies to plan for risk and control it as much as possible. This lesson discusses sources of risk and four basic ways to deal with it.

Objectives

To identify the elements of a Risk Management Plan, you will:

4A **List and discuss sources of project risk and the four approaches to dealing with risk.**

Every project is different, so how can you guess where trouble is going to come from? No one has a crystal ball, but there are patterns you can use to identify sources of risk. Once identified, risk management planning will help you determine how to handle the risk in the most appropriate way.

Topic 4A

Project Risk

What is Risk?   *UNCERTAINTY!*

Murphy's Law says that, if things can go wrong, they will go wrong. Luckily, Murphy overstated things a bit. We can predict with a degree of certainty that, in life, some things will go wrong and others will go right.

The possibility that things will go wrong is called *risk*. From a project management point of view, the risk that matters is anything that might negatively impact the project's completion on time, within budget, and to the pre-defined quality level.

Risk:
Uncertainty. Things that can go wrong and negatively impact the cost, time, or quality of a project.

Sources of Risk

Managing risk begins with identifying potential sources of risk. Every project is different, so you can't look to history to tell you exactly where problems might occur. However, history does tell us that trouble arises from broad categories of problems. You can use these categories as guidelines for predicting problems in your project.

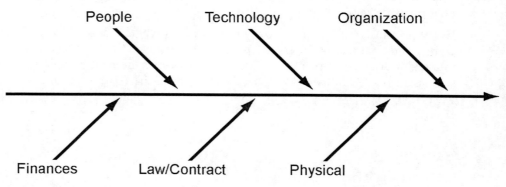

Figure 4-1: *Sources of risk.*

Project risk usually stems from the sources shown in Figure 4–1. The following table lists some questions you can use to pinpoint the type of risk that your project is exposed to.

Type of Risk	Questions to Ask
People	• Do you have the right skills on the team?
	• Will team members be available when needed?
	• Do they understand the project's purpose and objectives?
	• Can they work together?
Technology	• Does the team have access to the tools & software it needs?
	• Are the tools/software appropriate? robust? scalable?

Type of Risk	Questions to Ask
Organization	• Do all stakeholders agree on project objectives and purpose?
	• Are there stakeholders who have not participated in initiating the project?
	• Does the sponsor have enough clout to influence other stakeholders?
Finances	• Can the project manager require multiple signoffs before spending money? If so, how much time will they take and what is the scheduling impact?
	• Will currency fluctuations impact availability of cash?
	• Is ongoing funding dependent on timeliness of client's progress payments.
Law/Contract	• Are pending regulatory issues likely to impact project specifications?
	• Do our suppliers own the patent for the technology we expect to purchase?
Physical	• Are our workers more likely to get hurt if we increase the number of hours they work?
	• Will our existing noise-reduction devices protect workers from hearing damage?
Environment	• How will an early hurricane season impact our project?
	• Will dust from the neighboring factory impact our clean room air quality?
	• Will municipal construction projects impact our productivity?

TYPE OF RISK
- MISC: ODD ACTIVITIES THAT COULD OCCUR
- ACTS OF GOD

TASK 4A-1

Identifying Sources of Risk

Objective: Identify sources of risk in a project.

Setup: Based on what you know so far about the Italian Cookbook project, brainstorm some potential sources of risk.

1. **What are some potential risks for this project?**

Risk Assessment : USE SCALES

You probably do risk assessment every day, although you may not realize it. Do you take an umbrella to work if it looks like it might rain? Then you have assessed the *probability of risk* and decided that it was high enough to act upon. Do you leave your umbrella in the car if you are parked near the mall entrance? Then you have assessed the *impact* of the risk and decided that its consequences would not be too serious.

On a given project, there are a number of risks to assess. Figure 4–2 below shows a way to categorize and prioritize risks. You may wish to deal differently with risks that fall in the High Probability/High Impact category, as opposed to those that fall in the Low Probability/Low Impact category.

Probability of risk:
Likelihood that a problem
will occur

Impact of risk:
Degree of seriousness of the
risk's consequences.

RISK ASSESSMENT:

— QUALITATIVE

— QUANTITIVE!

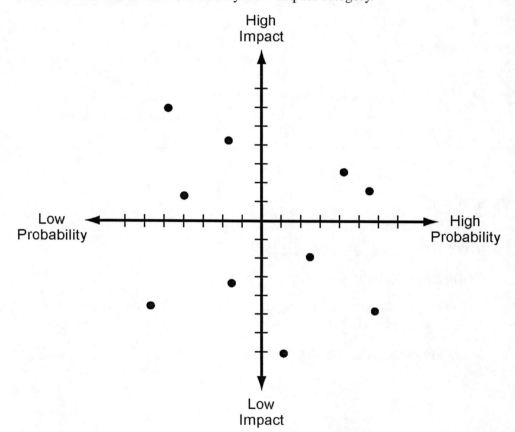

Figure 4-2: *Risk prioritization chart.*

TASK 4A-2

Assessing Risks

Objective: Assess the probability and impact of identified risks.

Setup: Refer to the flip chart answers from the previous scenario.

1. **How would you categorize each answer in regard to probability and impact on the project?**

Risk Management Approaches

Each project is unique and has a unique set of risks that beset it. However, no matter what the project, there are four basic approaches to managing risk:

- Avoid it. Find a work-around so that the risk never occurs.
- Accept it. Decide to live with the consequences, should they occur.
- Transfer it. Get someone else to share the risk or underwrite it for you.
- Mitigate it. Prepare to deal with the risk through contingency planning.

TASK 4A-3

Identifying Risk Management Approaches

1. The lead chef is known to have a heart condition. The publishers are concerned that their investment may be lost if the lead chef cannot complete the book due to health problems. Their plan: buy a "key man" policy that insures them against loss if the lead chef becomes ill or dies.

   What type of risk management approach is this?

   TRANSFER

2. The authors are concerned that readers may not be able to find authentic ingredients outside of Italy. Their plan: limit the ingredients to items that can be found in a typical U.S. supermarket.

   What type of risk management approach is this?

3. The publishers are concerned that the cookbook will be too short. Their plan: If the first draft seems too short by a few pages, add additional photo; if it is too short by 20 pages, add additional white space in the margins and increase the font size. If it is too short by more than 20 pages, resubmit it to the authors and request additional recipes.

   What type of risk management approach is this?

4. The authors are concerned that beginning cooks may not know common cooking techniques like how to baste a roast or how to whip cream. Their plan: Assume that most of their readers are advanced-level cooks who will know how to perform these techniques.

   What type of risk management approach is this?

Summary

One of the challenges of project management is identifying potential risks. Although you cannot predict exactly what will go wrong in a project, you can use pre-existing categories of risk to help you identify where the land mines in your project may be. Once identified, the risk should be assessed for probability and magnitude. Based on those assessments, you can prioritize the risk and plan strategies to deal with it. Traditionally, the four strategies are: avoiding, mitigating, transferring, and accepting the risk.

Apply Your Knowledge 4-1

Suggested Time:
5 minutes

Objective: Use a Risk Management Worksheet to identify sources of risk, assess the risk, and strategize about how to deal with it.

Instructions: Take a few moments to review this worksheet in your Project Portfolio. You will find a blank version on the CD-ROM that accompanies this book. The worksheet is meant to serve as a template. Use it with your stakeholders and project teams to help identify sources of risk in your project.

Lesson Review

4A List the four basic approaches to handling risk.   p.45

- AVOID IT
  - WORK AROUND So RISK NEVER OCCURS
- ACCEPT IT
  - LIVE w/ CONSEQUENCES
- TRANSFER IT
  - SHARE THE RISK
- MITIGATE IT
  - PREPARE TO DEAL w/ RISK

Project Plans

Overview

"If you fail to plan, you plan to fail."

In the Planning Phase of the project management life cycle, you specify what you need do to achieve your project objectives and decide in what sequence the steps must be done. The outputs from these activities — the Work Breakdown Structure and the network logic diagram — become the basic inputs you'll need to estimate time and cost for your project. They also become the team's guidelines during the Implementation and Close-Out Phases of the project.

Data Files
L5dpndcy.doc

Lesson Time
50-60 Minutes

Objectives

In order to plan project activities, you will:

5A **Identify the elements of the Work Breakdown Structure and the role this document plays in project planning.**

Creating a Work Breakdown Structure is one of the major activities during the Planning Phase. This document is a primary planning tool that is used and re-used throughout the project. It's the basis for much of the budgeting and resource planning that must be done later in the Planning Phase. It also serves as an input to scheduling.

5B **Discuss techniques for sequencing work packages and documenting the sequence.**

Using the Work Breakdown Structure, you identified all of the major subprojects that needed to be done in order to achieve the project objective, and you broke them into logical tasks or work packages. Next, you must create a logical sequence in which the tasks should be performed.

Topic 5A

The Work Breakdown Structure

Purpose of the Work Breakdown Structure

During the Planning Phase, you will construct a series of cascading plans. The top-level plan is called the *Work Breakdown Structure* (*WBS*). This plan summarizes all of the project's sub-projects and tasks, and displays them in a hierarchy. (See Figure 5–1) The WBS:

- Allows you to break out sub-projects which must be accomplished in order to complete the project.
- Helps you to visualize the sequence in which work must be performed.
- Allows you break out logical building blocks of activities called *work packages,* which can be used in assigning, estimating, scheduling, and controlling the work in your project.

Work Breakdown Structure (WBS):
Chart breaking down milestones and tasks that must be accomplished in a project.

Work Packages:
Detailed tasks and/or sub-tasks that can be used in assigning, estimating, scheduling, and controlling project work.

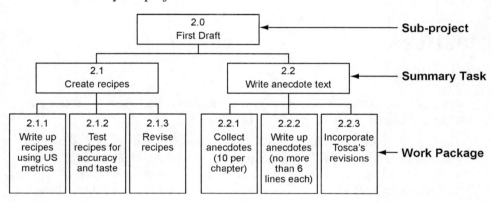

Figure 5-1: *Work Breakdown Structure (hierarchy format).*

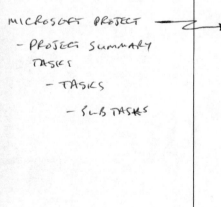

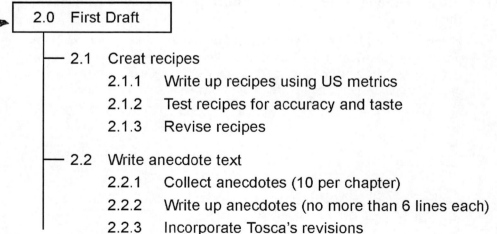

2.0   First Draft

— 2.1   Creat recipes
      2.1.1   Write up recipes using US metrics
      2.1.2   Test recipes for accuracy and taste
      2.1.3   Revise recipes

— 2.2   Write anecdote text
      2.2.1   Collect anecdotes (10 per chapter)
      2.2.2   Write up anecdotes (no more than 6 lines each)
      2.2.3   Incorporate Tosca's revisions

Figure 5-2: *Work Breakdown Structure (tree format).*

Elements and Levels of the WBS

You can construct the Work Breakdown Structure in an organizational chart-type hierarchy (see Figure 5–1) or in an outline–tree format (see Figure 5–2). Whichever format you choose, be sure to include these elements:

- The project objective or goal.
- The major sub-projects.
- Summary tasks for each milestone
- Detailed tasks, also known as *work packages*. Make sure these are worded so as to be measurable.

You should break sub-projects, summary tasks and detailed tasks into as many levels of detail as you will need in order to plan staffing, budget, or scheduling requirements. However, don't attempt to do a step-by-step procedure for how you will accomplish each sub-project or summary task. Here are some rules of thumb:

- If your summary task breaks down into eight or more work packages, the summary task is going to be too difficult to manage. If you really need all of those work packages, then consider breaking the summary task into two or more discrete summary tasks.
- Some people say that, if a work package takes less than a half day to complete, it may be too detailed. Consider consolidating it with a higher level task.
- The 8/80 rule says that, if a task is shorter than 8 hours or longer than 80 hours, it should be adjusted.
- One more rule: If breaking these rules of thumb makes it easier to plan or do your project, then disregard the rule.

The WBS is a living document. It may take a number of adjustments to get it just right to begin with. Later in the project, if new tasks are required to address changed objectives, you will have to make additions to the original WBS. Therefore, if you can, use a computer to create the WBS. You can use word processing, flow charting, or project management software to create a WBS.

Who Should Create the WBS?

The project's core team will use the WBS work packages for estimating, scheduling, and staffing the project. Therefore, rather than imposing the WBS on the team, get them involved in its creation. Participating in creating the WBS will help the team to bond around a common set of goals, clarify who is doing what on the project, and provide the team with a sense of project ownership, as well as foster a greater sense of commitment to meeting deadlines, budgets, and quality measures.

Work Packages:
Detailed tasks that must be performed in a project. The Work Package should include a statement of performance criteria.

If these rules don't fit your project, disregard them.

The WBS helps to make sure you include all the pieces of your project in your plan. However, if you do forget something, you can add it to your WBS later.

After the WBS is complete, your team should assign the work packages to individual work package owners. The <u>assignment should include</u> enough detail so that the work package owner and others on the team <u>understand the success criteria</u> for the work package. Items in the work package assignment should include:

- Task name
- Task description
- Task deliverables
- Measurement criteria
- Assumptions or constraints

Make sure to get agreement and sign-off on each work package from the work package owner. You should also get sign-off from team members who will be "customers" for the work package.

TASK 5A-1

Creating a WBS

Objective: Break down a summary task into detailed tasks.

Setup: The Italian Cookbook team knows that they are expected to create a final draft of the book before their project is complete. They also know that the final draft will include the incorporation of revised recipes and photos, and creating an attractive page layout. Finally, all of this must be assembled and proofread.

1. **What is the sub-project in this example?**

2. **What are the summary tasks?**

3. **List some work packages that make up the summary task for "incorporate revised photos."**

4. **Check your work: Have you included all necessary work packages in the summary task?** To check, make sure that all of the detailed tasks add up to the summary task.

5. **Check your work: Are your work packages measurable?** Make sure you include some criteria to indicate when the detailed task is considered complete.

6. How might you use your completed WBS to assign task owners or identify resources needed?

7. How might you use the WBS in Risk Management planning?

Topic 5B

Work Package Sequencing

Dependencies

In the WBS, you identified work packages. Before you can schedule them, you must arrange the work packages in logical sequence. Identifying this logical sequence is also known as identifying *dependencies*. There are four types of dependency relationships.

Relationship	Description
Finish-to-Start	The preceding activity must finish before the successor activity can start.
Finish-to-Finish	The preceding activity must finish before the successor activity can finish.
Start-to-Start	The preceding activity must start before the successor activity can start.
Start-to-Finish	The preceding activity must start before the successor activity can finish.

Some dependencies are necessarily logical. For example, if you must use the output of Task A to begin Task B, then the Finish-to-Start dependency relationship between the tasks is considered a *mandatory dependency*.

Other dependencies may be *discretionary*. For example, if you logically could do either Task A or Task B first, but your Project Sponsor wants to show the output of Task A to the Stakeholder Team as soon as possible, than discretionary dependency will determine your sequencing.

dependencies:
Relationships among work packages that determine the sequence in which work should be performed.

mandatory dependency:
a dependency relationship in which there is only one logical sequence of activities.

discretionary dependency:
a dependency relationship which is imposed due to organizational preference or other optional criterion.

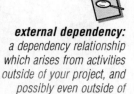

It is also possible to have *external* dependencies, or dependencies which arise because of something outside of the project. For example, if you can't do Task B until an international standards organization publishes its next iteration of product standards, then Task B is subject to an external dependency.

As you sort through a project's worth of work packages, you will find it difficult to keep track of dependency relationships. A good tool for keeping organized is a Dependency Table, like the following.

ID	Task	Predecessors	Resources Needed
1	Write recipes		Tosca, writer
2	Test recipes	1	Chef, Asst. chef, Tosca
3	Revise recipes	2	Tosca, writer, chef, asst. chef
4	Lay out pages	3	Graphic artist
5	Take photos	3	Photographer, food stylist
6	Write introduction		Writer

(handwritten margin notes: F/S beside row 2, F/S beside row 3, S/F beside row 6)

The Network Logic Diagram

After you have identified dependencies, use them to construct a *network logic diagram*. This diagram will become one of the key planning, organizing, and controlling tools in your project management arsenal. It shows you—and your team—the "big picture" of your project activities. You can use it to plan initial schedules and budgets. Later in the project, you can use it to deal with scope changes, requests to accelerate the schedule or lower the budget, etc. You can also use it to monitor and control deviation from your plans.

There are a variety of network logic diagramming conventions, but the most common today is called Precedence Diagramming Method (PDM). In a PDM network logic diagram, rectangular nodes represent activities. Connecting arrows represent dependencies. Nodes which are parallel but unconnected to one another are nondependent and can occur at the same time.

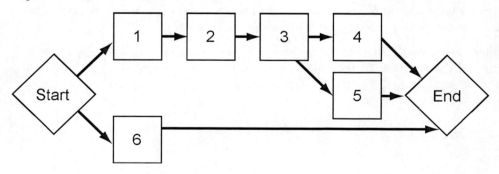

Figure 5-3: *Network logic diagram.*

TASK 5B-1

Using a Network Logic Diagram

Objective: Create nodes on a network logic diagram and interpret what the diagram is telling you.

Setup: Refer to Figure 5–3 to answer the questions.

1. Assuming that we are diagramming tasks to show Finish-to-Start dependencies, what task must be completed before Task 5 begins?

2. What tasks could be done at the same time as Task 1? Must they be done at the same time as Task 1?

3. An additional task, Task 7, has been added. It can't begin until Task 6 is completed. Task 5 is dependent on Task 7. Draw Task 7 where it belongs on Figure 5–3.

Before You Move On

The WBS and the network logic diagram are time-consuming to create. However, they are the building blocks for all of your scheduling and estimating activities for the project. Your team will find them invaluable during the Implementation Phase as they complete project activities. They also serve as valuable Control tools. So invest some time in the early phases to get these tools done right!

Summary

The Work Breakdown Structure and the network logic diagram are two tools that help you plan your project activities. The Work Breakdown Structure shows project work packages, breaks down the summary activities needed to achieve each work package, and then breaks down the detailed activities needed to achieve each summary activity. On the network logic diagram, detailed activities (also called work packages) are displayed to show dependency relationships among the work packages. The dependency relationships will dictate the order in which work must be scheduled in the project.

Suggested Time:

15 minutes

Apply Your Knowledge 5-1

Instructions: Take a few moments to review this worksheet in your Project Portfolio. You will find a blank version on the CD-ROM that accompanies this book. Use the Dependency Table worksheet to list a few tasks in your project and determine dependencies among the tasks. If time permits, sketch a network logic diagram to show the dependency relationships.

Lesson Review

5A   Arrange these elements of a WBS into hierarchical order:

___   Summary tasks

___   Major sub-projects

___   Work packages

___   Project objective

5B   Sequencing in which a task must be completed before the next task can begin is called

___   a. Start to Finish

___   b. Start to Start

___   c. Finish to Finish

___   d. Finish to Start

Which tool lists summary activities, and then breaks them down into detailed activities or work packages?

Which tool helps you visualize the dependency relationships among work packages?

The Project Schedule

Data Files
L6AYK.doc

Lesson Time
60-75 minutes

Overview

A famous economist "Work expands to fill the time available for its completion." — C. Northcote Parkinson, economist.

As a project manager, you have to control time or it will control you. That is why project scheduling is a critical activity for any project. This lesson will show you how to estimate time, calculate initial schedules, and find the Critical Path for your project.

Objectives

In order to identify the Critical Path for completing a project on schedule, you will:

6A   **Discuss the activities that occur during the scheduling process and the reasons for including the project team in scheduling.**

This section overviews the steps in the scheduling process and the benefits of including the project team in scheduling activities.

6B   **Discuss how to derive time estimates for activities on the network logic diagram.**

After dependencies are identified and network logic diagrams have been created, your team can estimate the amount of time to complete each work package. It is important that every team member use common terms and units to describe work effort.

Topic 6A

The Scheduling Process

Scheduling Steps

Scheduling is the process of estimating the time needed to do work on a project, and creating the most efficient timetable to accomplish the work. Inputs to the scheduling process are identifying work packages, sequencing them, and displaying their dependency relationships on a network logic diagram.

The scheduling process includes these steps:

- Estimating the <u>duration</u> and effort for each work package
- Calculating the <u>Critical Path</u>, or set of activities that cannot be delayed, in order to accomplish project work on time.
- Calculating activities that have <u>float</u>, or additional time, during which resources can be assigned to help accomplish Critical Path activities.

Who Should Be Involved?

Earlier you learned that the WBS should be a team effort, so that team members would buy in to the project's purpose and goals. At the end of WBS activity, individual team members were assigned responsibility for each work package in the WBS.

Now, you will use the information from the WBS to perform scheduling activities. As you arrange work packages into logical sequence and estimate the amount of effort it will take to complete each work package, the team needs to be involved once again. Why? From a data integrity point of view, your schedule will be more accurate if it is based on estimates from the people who are closest to the individual tasks. From a team commitment point of view, team members will be more likely to commit to meeting a schedule if they had input into it.

Topic 6B

Time Estimates

Work Effort

After your team has created the network logic diagram, estimate the time it will take to complete each work package. Frequently, each work package owner is asked to create an initial estimate for that work package, and then share it with the team. To avoid confusion, it's important for all the team members to use the same approach to calculating time:

DURATION: DAYS OR WEEKS
* 1 DAY

WORK: PEOPLE HOURS
* 8 HRS/DAY

UNITS:
* 100% OF 8 HRS/DAY

EFFORT DRIVEN:
    MORE RESOURCES USED
    MEANS LESS TIME.

    16 HRS/DAY → 2 PEOPLE

- ELAPSE DURATION:
    TIME FOR PAINT
    TO DRY

Term	Definition
Task Time	The amount of labor or resource time it will take to do the activities in the task. Sometimes referred to as "work effort" or "billable hours."
Duration of Effort	The total time needed to complete the task, including waiting times. Sometimes referred to as "elapsed time."

task time:
The amount of labor or resource time it will take to complete the activities in a task.

duration of effort:
The total time needed to complete a task, including waiting times.

Here is an example that should help to distinguish the two concepts. Let's say that it takes a chef 24 hours to create the perfect Marinara Sauce: 8 hours to prepare the ingredients and cook the sauce, and the remaining 16 hours to cool the sauce and let all the flavors meld. The *task time* to create the Marinara Sauce is 8 hours. The *duration of effort* is 24 hours.

Now, let's say that you cut the cooking time in half by assigning a second chef to the task. Your task time becomes 2@4 hours. The duration of effort becomes 20 hours.

When your team estimates time, they need to estimate both task time and duration of effort. If they adjust their duration of effort estimate based on number of people assigned, they need to provide you with those labor assumptions. Capture this information on a chart like the one in Figure 6–1. You will use their duration of effort numbers to prepare your project schedule. (You will learn how to use the work effort number in Lesson 7, The Project Budget.)

Project Work Package Estimation Table
Use this worksheet to document the time estimates made by your team.

ID #	Task	Duration (days)	Task Time	Resources
1				
2				
3				
4				
5				
6				
7				
8				
9				

Figure 6-1: *Estimation table.*

Here are some additional tips for estimating time:

- Ask everyone on the team to <u>use the same units of time</u>. Depending on the project, choose minutes, hours, days, or weeks.

- If necessary, <u>break work packages into sub-tasks</u> for estimating purposes.

- If similar tasks appear in more than one work package, try to work out a <u>standard estimate and apply it uniformly</u>.

- Don't be afraid to use history as a guide for estimating. <u>Seek confirmation</u> of task estimates from experienced people or look back at previous projects.

Schedule Calculations

With a completed network logic diagram and duration estimates, you can begin to put together your schedule. Typically, you will have a start date and a finish date in mind. Your challenge will be to schedule tasks so they can be accomplished between those two fixed points. To do this, you must first find the network path that has the longest overall duration. This network path is called the *critical path*. You cannot delay any activities on the critical path or your project as a whole will be late.

However, you haven't looked at the total picture yet. In order to do a more intelligent job of scheduling, you need to know the earliest possible start and finish times for each activity , as well as the latest possible start and finish times for each activity. To calculate the Early Start/Late Start (ES/LS) and Early Finish/Late Finish (EF/LF), you perform *forward pass* and *backward pass* calculations. By subtracting ES from LS, or EF from LF, you can determine the *float*, or slack time, you have available. This will also tell you the activities in which the float will occur. By knowing where the float is, you can do a better job of managing your resources over the course of your project.

Here are some terms you will need to know in order to calculate the critical path:

Short Form	Term	Definition
DU	Duration	Running time duration of an activity
ES	Early Start	Earliest running time in which an activity can begin
LS	Late Start	Latest running time in which an activity can begin
EF	Early Finish	Earliest running time in which an activity can end
LS	Late Finish	Latest running time in which an activity can end

Project Management software will automate the schedule calculations for you. However, by learning to understand the calculation logic, you will be able to validate your computerized schedule and adjust it to your needs.

Critical Path:
Network path with the longest total duration. Items on the critical path cannot be delayed or the project as a whole will be late.

LARGEST

Forward Pass:
Calculating the Early Start and Early Finish times for project work

SMALLEST

Backwards Pass:
Calculating the Late Start and Late Finish times for project work

Float:
Extra time available to do a task

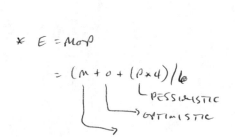

$$\ast \quad E = MoP$$
$$= (M + o + (P \times 4))/6$$

PESSIMISTIC

OPTIMISTIC

As you complete these calculations, you enter them in the network logic diagram. Figure 6–2 shows a network logic diagram that has been drawn with labeled areas to capture these values as they are calculated.

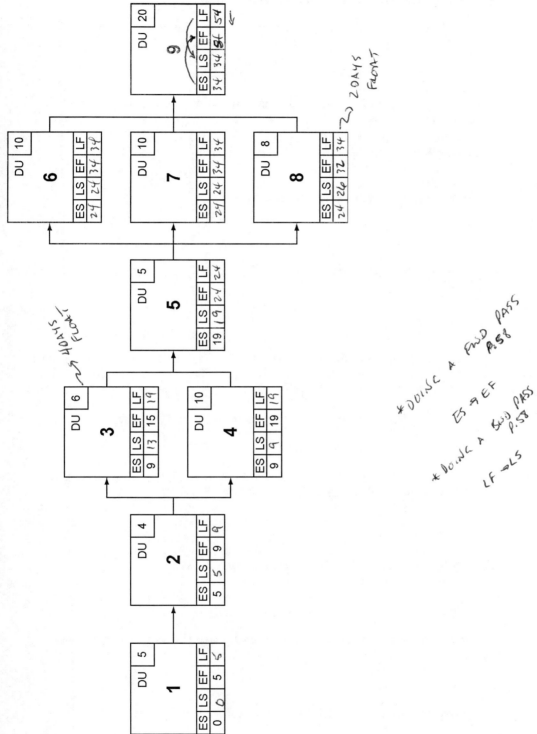

Figure 6-2: *Network diagram.*

TASK 6B-1

Finding the Critical Path and Float

Objective: Network Logic DiagramIdentify the critical path and float for a set of tasks.

Setup: Refer to Figure 6–2 as you work through this Task.

1.   **Calculate the path through the network that has the longest overall duration.** For example, Nodes 1 + 2 + 3 + 5 + 6 + 10 have a cumulative duration of 50 days. If you choose to take the path of Nodes 1 + 2 + 4 + 5 + 6 + 9, the duration is 54 days. The path with the longest duration is the Critical Path.

2.   **What happens if Node 4 is delayed?**

   What happens if Node 3 is delayed?

3.   **Next, we begin our forward pass.** In Node 1, the duration is estimated to be 5 hours. The early start time is at 0 hours – because you can start this task at the beginning of the project. The early finish time is at 5 hours.

   Why does the earliest finish time have to be at 5 hours?

4.   **What is the earliest start time for Node 2? Why?**

5.   **What is the earliest finish time for Node 2? Why?**

6.   **The early start times for Nodes 3 and 4 are the same. Why?**

7.   **What are the early finish times for Nodes 3 and 4? Why?**

8.   **Notice that the early start date for Node 5 is 19.** In a forward pass calculation, if more than one node precedes a node, use the latest early finish date from the preceding nodes.

9. **Complete the forward pass calculation for the other nodes.**

Your forward pass calculation shows that it will take a minimum of 54 hours to do the tasks on the network logic diagram. Now let's do a backwards pass calculation.

10. **Now for the backwards pass calculation.**

In Node 9, **enter 54 in the Late Finish box.** In other words, if we accept the way this diagram is drawn, the project can't end later than 54 hours after it began.

11. **Calculate the Late Start by subtracting the duration from the Late Finish. Enter the amount (34) in the Late Start box for Node 9.**

12. **What are the Late Start and Late Finish amounts for Nodes 6, 7, and 8?**

13. **Now you have a problem. What should the Late Finish of Node 5 be, and why?**

14. **What are the LS and LF amounts for all other nodes on the diagram?**

15. **Now we can identify float.**

Find each node in which either its ES is different from its LS, or its EF is different from its LF. You will see this in Nodes 3 and 8 on our diagram. These represent activities in which you have some leeway as to when the activities must be scheduled. You still have to do these tasks, but the exact time at which you do them is not critical.

16. **Once you identify float, what can you do with this information?**

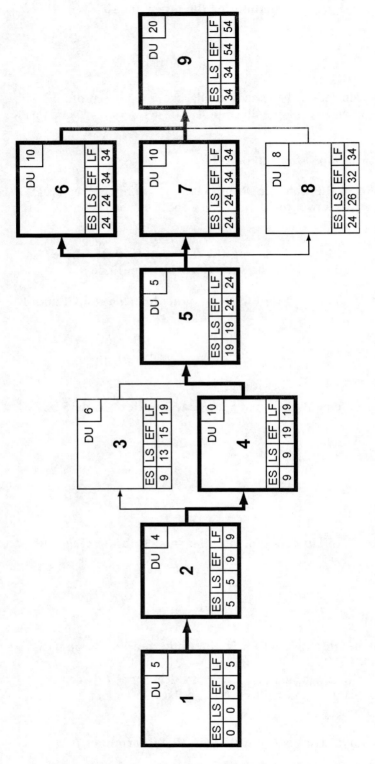

Figure 6-3: *Completed forward & backward pass calculations.*

Significance of Critical Path and Float

The Critical Path is the longest path through your network schedule. All activities on the critical path must be completed on time, or the entire schedule will slip. It is important for the entire project team to understand the Critical Path and float for the project.

Float time allows you some leeway. For example, if your Critical Path activities appear to be in danger of being delayed, you may wish to borrow some resources from the float activities to help get back on track. Remember that float hours are finite; once you use up a task's float hours, the task becomes part of the Critical Path.

Once you use up a task's float, the task becomes part of the Critical Path.

From Duration to Schedule

After you have calculated Critical Path, use your network logic diagram and calculations to create a calendar-type schedule. For example, if you have a project implementation kick-off date of January 1, then January 1 becomes the early start date for first work package in your network. Use duration and dependency information to schedule in the rest of the time. A Gantt Chart (see Figure 6–4) is the best way to display the schedule information.

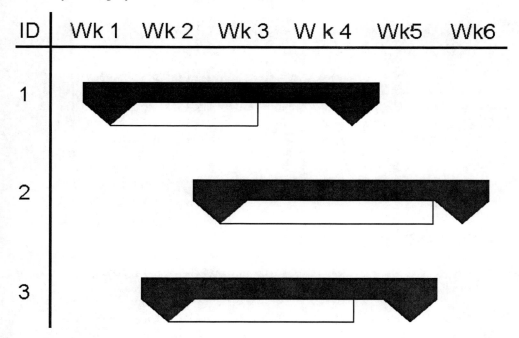

Figure 6-4: *Gantt chart.*

What do you do if your schedule runs longer than the project's predetermined end date? Revisit each work package on the critical path, but this time look at the duration time, task time and resources assigned. Ask yourself: If we used more resources, could we shorten the duration? What effect does this have on task time? Recalculate your Critical Path and redraw your Gantt Chart accordingly.

Benefits of Software

Once you understand the concepts of Critical Path and float, and how they are derived, you may wish to consider using project management software to automate these calculations. These programs allow you to:

- Automate the transfer of the Critical Path's duration-based calculations to a calendar schedule.
- Reschedule to accommodate a different project completion date.
- Compare different resource utilization options.
- Display different schedule views, such as Network Logic Diagram and Gantt Chart views for portions of your project or the entire project.

Don't assume that adding resources will cut duration without affecting task time. Sometimes, adding more people makes the task more difficult and therefore more time-consuming.

If you would like to inquire about Element K's Project Management software courses, please ask your instructor for information.

Gantt Chart views may be easier for stakeholders and other interested parties to understand. Some project managers use Gantt Charts for presentation and keep the Network Logic Diagrams for detailed analysis.

Suggested Time:
5 minutes

Summary

Scheduling is one of the most critical activities in project management and should involve the entire project team. Scheduling activities include: estimating duration and task time, creating a network logic diagram that shows task dependencies, identifying the project's critical path, conducting forward and backwards pass calculations to determine Early Start/Late Start and Early Finish/ Late Finish, and identifying float time. Project management software can help automate these activities, making it easier for the project manager to accommodate schedule changes over the course of the project.

Apply Your Knowledge 6-1

Objective: Use the Schedule Estimation Worksheets to collect and document estimating and schedule information.

Instructions: Take a few moments to review this worksheet in your Project Portfolio. You will find a blank version on the CD-ROM that accompanies this book. The worksheet is meant to serve as a template. Use it with your project team to collect and document schedule-related estimates.

Lesson Review

6A Why should the project team participate in the scheduling process?

_____ a. Team participation is likely to make the scheduling process go faster.

_____ b. Team participation allows individuals who are closer to the actual tasks to be responsible for estimating the duration of the task.

_____ c. Individuals are more likely to commit to meeting a deadline if they participated in setting it.

6B In order to calculate the critical path, in what order must you do these activities?

_____ Perform forwards and backwards pass calculations

_____ Identify activities with float

_____ Assign duration estimates to each node on the network logic diagram

The Project Budget

LESSON
7

Data Files
L7AYK.doc

Lesson Time
50-60 minutes

Overview

"Time is money."

So far, you have planned work activities and created a preliminary schedule that will allow your team to accomplish its goals within the project's time constraints. But the project has cost constraints, too. Now, your challenge is to determine the cost of planned activities, and to budget so your project meets its predetermined cost constraints.

Objectives

In order to list the elements of a budget and describe how they are derived, you will:

7A **List and discuss the cost elements that should be included in a budget.**

Part of your planning activity is to estimate the cost to do all of the activities in your project. In this section, you will learn what items should be included in every budget.

7B **Discuss techniques for deriving cost estimates from work packages**

When you broke your project into work packages and analyzed the activities you would need to perform, you began the budgeting process. This section will tell you how to apply some of that earlier data to estimate project costs.

7C **Discuss how to bring budgets and schedules into line with project goals.**

After preliminary scheduling and cost estimating is complete, the results have to align with your project's time, cost, and quality criteria.

Topic 7A

What is a Budget?

The Project Budget

A *project budget* is a plan for how you will spend money on a project. Its purpose is to estimate the amount of money that will be needed for the project, and when it will be needed. (As you will learn in the next chapter, a good budget is a useful control tool, too.) It should reflect all of the labor, overhead, and expenses expected for the project. Since Murphy's Law operates overtime on projects, project budgets may also contain a contingency or management reserve to cover unexpected expenses.

project budget:
A plan for how you will spend money on each work package in a project.

Project budgets often contain a contingency or management reserve to protect against overruns.

From Cost Estimate to Budget

The budgeting process starts with cost estimates. The cost elements in the following table appear in most estimates, although they may be called by different names. Work with the financial specialist on your team to use the terminology and categories that match your internal accounting procedures:

Cost Element	Description	Formula
Labor	The cost of the people working on the project. Include expected overtime. May include overhead and fringe benefits, depending on the organization. Both formulae are shown at right.	• Regular hours × hourly rate) + (overtime hours × overtime rate) • Regular hcurs X hourly rate) + (overtime hours × overtime rate) + pro-rated overhead and fringe benefits • For contract labor, use hourly and overtime rates only
Equipment	The purchase, lease, or rental price, and the cost of usage	• Purchase price • Lease or rental price × time period • Pro-rated usage fees
Facilities	The cost of space to house your team, provide electric and phone service, etc.	• Rental cost × time period • Organizational burden rate × time period
Supplies	The consumables your team will use during the project.	• Estimated volume × (cost + inflation adjustment)
Special expenses	Specialized services, miscellaneous items, etc.	• Estimated cost of service or items

Labor is usually the biggest component of the cost estimate. It's important to include all labor costs, even if you are sharing employees whose salaries are paid by their functional organizations. Factoring in their labor costs is the only way that you can determine the cost of your project.

TASK 7A-1

Identifying Cost Elements

> **Objective:** Identify and classify cost elements
>
> **Setup:** Use your knowledge of the Italian Cookbook Case Study to answer these questions.

1. **Give a specific example of each cost category and explain how you would compute it. (Example: Labor: Assistant chefs (2) × # hours and overtime hours in each work package**

Topic 7B

Creating a Preliminary Budget

Task Time Revisited

During your activity planning and scheduling work, you broke out the task time and duration time for each work package. You used duration time to create a schedule. Now you can use task time to create your cost estimate.

TASK 7B-1

Converting Task Time Data to Cost Estimates

Objective: Use task time data to estimate labor costs.

1. **Review the two tables. Follow the flow of data from one table to the next.**

ID	Task	Dur Time	Task Time	Resources
2	Test recipes	10 wks	10 wks	• Chef (10 wks, 50 hrs/wk)
				• Asst. chef (10 wks, 50 hrs/wk)
				• Tosca (10 days)
5	Photograph recipes	2 wks	1 wk	• Photographer (5 days, 8 hrs/day)
				• Food stylist (10 day contract)

ID	Resource	Total Hrs	OT Hrs	Rate (Reg)	Rate (OT)	Total Cost
2	Asst. Chef	400	100	$20	$30	
5	Photographer	40	0	$50	$75	

2. **In the Test Recipes work package, you expect to need an assistant chef for 10 weeks. You expect that the assistant chef will work 10 hours a day, from Monday to Friday. An assistant chef's hourly rate is $20/hr for an 8–hour day. Standard Publishing's overtime rate is time-and-a-half. Calculate the total labor cost estimate for the assistant chef's work in this work package.**

3. **In the Photograph Recipes work package, you expect to need a professional photographer on a one-day-a-week basis, from 9 to 5, for 4 weeks. A professional photographer's hourly rate is $50/hr for an 8 hour day. What is the total labor estimate for the photographer?**

Topic 7C

Budget and Schedule Balancing

Achieving a Balance

In the real world, you may find that your Critical Path takes longer than the allotted time to do the project. Or, you may find that your total cost estimate is higher than your predetermined budget goal.

Often, you can trade off between time and cost in order to meet project goals. If your preliminary schedule runs too long, but you have some budget room, you may be able to add overtime hours or additional people to shorten the schedule. Be careful to make these adjustments realistically. Ask yourself:

- Will adding overtime hours help, or are people stretched too thin already?

- Will adding additional people help, or is this a task in which adding additional people will complicate things to the point that time is not saved?

- What other costs am I adding? (For example, if I add an additional assistant chef, do I need additional kitchen facilities or equipment also?)

- Will these changes make it more difficult to meet quality goals?

Similarly, sometimes you can reduce your estimated costs by lengthening your schedule. For example, if you have one person working a 12–hour shift, you are paying for 8 hours of regular labor and 4 hours of overtime labor. For a $50/hour job, that's $700. If the work package is not on the critical path, you may wish to use up some of your float time and do the same job for 12 regular labor hours, or $600. Once again, be sure to ask some questions before revising the budget:

- Am I adjusting an activity that is on the Critical Path? If so, can the project survive with a lengthened schedule?

- Am I adding new costs by revising the schedule? (For example, if I reduce the number of overtime hours and lengthen the schedule, will additional equipment rental costs offset my labor cost savings?)

- Will these changes make it more difficult to meet quality goals?

What happens if both the budget and schedule are out of line, and can't be brought into line with initial project goals? First, check to make sure no scope creep has occurred. If all the project work is in scope, share your findings with your sponsor. The project goals may need to be renegotiated, and the stakeholders may need to prioritize time, cost, and quality criteria for the project.

You can trade off among cost, time, or quality to achieve the proper balance for your project. Remember that changing any of the three success factors will impact all of them.

SCHEDULE CRASHING:

SCHEDULE COMPRESSION:
LOOKING @ EXISTING
RELATIONSHIPS TO
ADJUST SCHEDULE

TASK 7C-1

Balancing the Schedule and Budget

Objective: Discuss adjusting a schedule or budget to align with project goals.

1. Use the data in the table below to answer these questions.

ID	Resource	Total Hrs	OT Hrs	Rate (Reg)	Rate (OT)	Total Cost
2	Asst. Chef	400	100	$20	$30	$9,000
5	Photographer	40	0	$50	$75	$2,000

2. **You need to reduce the labor cost for work package #2. Do you see a way to eliminate some of the cost? How might your strategy affect cost, time, and quality?**

3. **You need to shorten the work schedule. You are considering hiring two photographers, and reducing the task time for each one to 20 hours. What tools might you use when you make this decision? What is the likely impact on time, cost, and quality?**

Completing the Project Plans

When you have balanced the budget and schedule, you may wish to edit your Work Breakdown Structure, network logic diagram, and other deliverables from the Planning Phase. Submit a summary version of the Planning milestone deliverables (see Figure 7–1) to your sponsor and stakeholders for approval before continuing on to the next phase of the project.

PHASE	DELIVERABLES

PLANNING

Budgeting

Scheduling

Activity Planning

Deliverables Breakdown Structure

Work Breakdown Structure

Detailed Responsibility Matrix

Schedule

Budget

Activity Plan

Figure 7-1: *Planning phase and deliverables.*

Summary

Budgeting, or planning how money will be spent in a project, is an important part of the Planning Phase of a project. In a preliminary budget, the project team estimates the total cost of labor, equipment, facilities, supplies, and special expenses. Labor costs often account for the largest portion of the total project budget. After a preliminary cost estimate, the team may need to re-align the schedule and budget to meet time, cost, and quality goals.

Apply Your Knowledge 7-1

Objective: Use worksheets to collect the task time estimates you will need for budgeting and resource planning.

Instructions: Use these two worksheets to help estimate time per work package, and then determine labor cost for each resource in each work package. (Blank copies of the worksheets are provided on your CD-ROM.)

Lesson Review

7A **What cost category is usually the biggest cost component in a project budget?**

7B **Which of these items is a true statement?**

_____ a. Labor rate multiplies hourly rate times regular hours, but should not include overtime.

_____ b. The hourly rate should be the same for all workers in a given work package.

_____ c. Labor estimates typically include labor costs for team members whose salaries are already being paid by other departments.

7C **You need to reduce your labor cost estimates by 10%. You know that your projected overtime costs account to 10% of the labor estimate. Name three factors you should examine before deciding to cut out the overtime.**

Project Tracking and Control  LESSON 8

Data Files
L8AYK.doc

Lesson Time
60-75 minutes

Overview

"If you are sure you understand everything that is going on, you are hopelessly confused." – Walter Mondale, 1978

Once a project gets underway, it seems to take on a life of its own. Team members, concentrating on their work package assignments, can easily lose track of how they are doing in terms of time, cost, and quality. During the Implementation Phase of the Project Management Life Cycle, the project manager must track the project's performance and take action, if necessary, to get it back on track.

Objectives

In order to discuss techniques for controlling for deviation from budgets and schedules, you will:

8A   Discuss issues in creating positive project momentum.

How do you set a project on the right track? What needs to be in place so that team members can do their work? This section deals with some of the issues that project managers must face in order to set the stage for successful project execution.

8B   Discuss baselining techniques for monitoring and communicating project progress.

This section shows you simple ways to monitor whether your project is meeting its time and cost goals and to convey that project status to others.

8C   Discuss the use of Earned Value Analysis in checking for deviation from schedules and budgets.

Earned Value Analysis is a method for monitoring project performance which takes both time and cost information into account simultaneously. It provides a more complete picture of project status than simple variance reporting.

8D   Discuss the importance of systematic monitoring and techniques for getting the project back on track.

Systematic monitoring is necessary to catch problems while there is still time to correct them. If projects go off track, the project manager may need to negotiate trade-offs between time, cost, and quality.

Topic 8A

Moving the Project Forward

The Implementation Phase

In the previous phases of the Project Management Life Cycle, you laid the groundwork for project success. You created detailed plans, schedules, and budgets – and your stakeholders accepted them. You worked with your team to assign the right people to each work package, you planned the tasks that made up each work package, and you delegated work package responsibility to the appropriate team members.

In the Implementation phase, the project manager has two important tasks: getting everyone the tools they need to succeed and monitoring project progress.

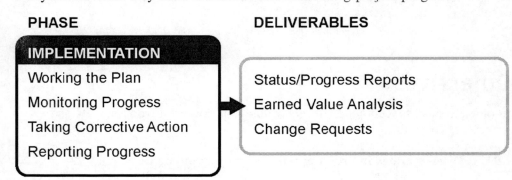

PHASE

IMPLEMENTATION

Working the Plan

Monitoring Progress

Taking Corrective Action

Reporting Progress

DELIVERABLES

Status/Progress Reports

Earned Value Analysis

Change Requests

Figure 8-1: *Implementation phase.*

The Tools to Succeed

The project manager must put processes in place so team members have what they need, when they need it:

- Access to resources (people, equipment, supplies)
- Access to information (status reports, technical data, external benchmarks)
- Access to training (specialized skill-building needed for project work)
- Access to expectations (plans, work package specifications, team rules)

Typically, the organization already has functional departments in charge of these chores. Sometimes the functional departments deliver a level of service that fits the project's needs, but sometimes they do not. The project manager must play the role of *boundary manager* , negotiating between those within the project and those outside of it, to get the project team the tools it needs.

At the same time, the project manager must work to resolve conflict within the team. As work gets underway, individuals may view their work package needs as all-important; they don't always see that others have equally legitimate needs that must be met to ensure project completion. The project manager helps team members deal with conflicting priorities and resolve differences that might get in the way of good team work.

boundary management:
Managing the interfaces between your functional or project area, and those outside it.

Finally, the project manager must act as a sort of cheerleader, maintaining project support at the executive and sponsor level, building camaraderie and can-do attitude at the team level, and providing feedback and guidance at the individual work package level.

TASK 8A-1

Discussing Boundary Management

1. From your organization, what is an example of a boundary management task that a project manager might be expected to perform?

Working through the sponsor can be politically sensitive. If your goal is to create a good long-term relationships with the functional manager, you may be better off to negotiate directly.

Topic 8B

Monitoring for Project Progress

Identifying Variances *(DIFFERENCE BETWEEN BASELINE & ACTUAL)*

As part of your planning, your team created specifications for each work package: schedule dates, cost estimates, and completion criteria. During the Implementation Phase, this data serves a two-fold purpose: for work package owners, it sets expectations and specifications; for the project manager, it acts as a benchmark for monitoring project progress.

The information you need to monitor a project is simple. For each work package, you need to ask your work package owners:

*   How much *time* has been spent to date?
*   How much *money* has been spent to date?
*   How complete is the work (0%, 50%, 100%)?

On a large project with many tasks happening simultaneously, this represents a lot of information. One way to keep the information organized is in a Status Chart (see Table below). It helps you to identify *variances* between planned and actual status. Variances can be negative or positive, depending on whether you are using less or more time or money than planned.

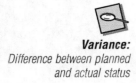

Variance:
Difference between planned and actual status

Status Chart Showing Budget Variances

Task	Budget to Date	Actual to Date	Budget Underrun	Budget Overrun	Total Budget	Estimated at End
6	$6,000	$5,000	$1,000		$7,500	$6,500
8	$10,000	$11,000		$1,000	$12,000	$13,000

Project Baselining

Sponsors, team members and other stakeholders need to understand your project status. A baseline chart (see Figure 8–2) shows schedule variances, in a format that most people can understand. The *project baseline* is your original schedule data, broken out by work package. The baseline doesn't change (unless you and your team decide to change the project goals). The *status data* reflects the current completion level of your project. Taken together, you get a direct, visual comparison of where you are and where you ought to be on any work package.

Project Baseline:
A snapshot of your original schedule and budget plans.

Status Data:
The current completion level of your project.

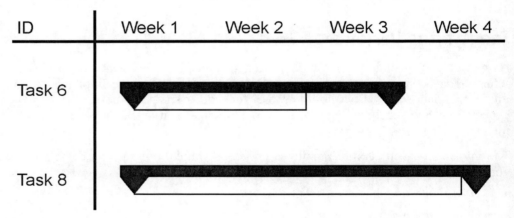

ID	Week 1	Week 2	Week 3	Week 4
Task 6				
Task 8				

Figure 8-2: *Baseline chart with actuals.*

Variances can also be displayed on a bar chart. In Figure 8–2, the chart shows actual versus estimated cost performance to date.

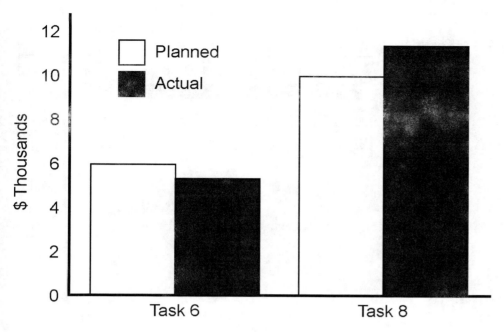

Figure 8-3: *Bar chart of actual versus estimated costs.*

TASK 8B-1

Using Variance Data

Objective: Use variance data to characterize project status.

Setup: Use the illustrations below to answer the questions.

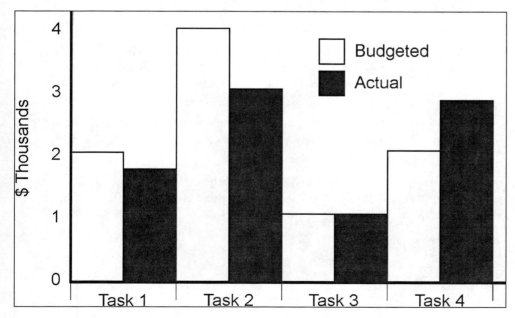

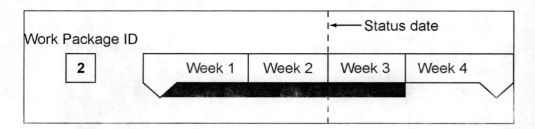

Work Package ID

2

| Week 1 | Week 2 | Week 3 | Week 4 |

Status date

1. **Based on the baseline chart, what is the schedule status of Work Package #2?**

2. **Based on the variance bar chart, what is the status of Task #4?**

Topic 8C

Earned Value Analysis

Beyond Variances

Variance information is simple to understand and easy to display, but doesn't tell the whole story about project performance. For example:

- Suppose that a work package is two weeks behind schedule. What does that tell you about the cost performance in that work package? Is the work package under budget, over budget, or on-estimate – and how can you tell, since your estimates were based on the cost to complete the work package?

- Suppose that a work package is under budget by four percent. Does that mean that the work is costing less than you estimated, or does it mean that you have received four percent less work than expected at this point in the schedule?

- Some work packages are behind schedule and some are ahead. Some work packages are under budget and some are above. How can you tell if the project is in trouble?

To really understand how your are doing on a project, you have to simultaneously capture both time and cost performance on the project. One way to do that is called Earned Value Analysis.

Variables used in Earned Value Analysis

Earned Value Analysis is a method for monitoring project progress which simultaneously measures both time and cost performance. In order to compute Earned Value, you first compute these variables:

Earned Value Analysis:
A method for monitoring project progress which measures both time and cost performance.

Acronym	Variable
BCWS	*Budgeted Cost for Work Scheduled.* (The amount you budgeted for a task between its start date and today. For example, say that you expected a task to take 10 days and cost $1000. Today is day 3. The BCWS on day 3 is $300.)
BCWP	*Budgeted Cost for Work Performed.* (Also known as *Earned Value.* The percentage of the task budget that corresponds to the tasks's completion status. For example, if the $1000 task is only 10% complete on day 3, its BCWP is $100)
ACWP	*Actual Cost for Work Performed.* (The actual cost of the task so far. For example, if you have spent $500 of your $1000 by day 3, the ACWP is $500.)

$100/DAY (handwritten annotation)

Budgeted Cost for Work Scheduled (BCWS):
Budgeted Cost for Work Scheduled. (The amount you budgeted for a task between its start date and today.

Budgeted Cost for Work Performed (BCWP):
Also known as Earned Value. The percentage of the task budget that corresponds to the tasks's completion status.

Earned Value:
Also known as Budgeted Cost for Work Performed. The percentage of the task budget that corresponds to the tasks's completion status.

You can compute the variables in Work Package, Task, or Project units, depending on what level you are monitoring.

Earned Value Calculations

Use the variables above to calculate variances that interrelated both cost and schedule.

Acronym	Variance	Calculation
CV	Cost Variance	BCWP — ACWP
SV	Schedule Variance	BCWP — BCWS

Both of these calculations will result in dollar units, which are not too useful in expressing schedule variances. Therefore, one more series of calculations is needed to express both cost and schedule variances in terms of percentages.

Acronym	Variance	Calculation
CVP	Cost Variance Percentage. Divides cost variance by budgeted cost. A negative value means a cost overrun.	CV÷BCWP
SVP	Schedule Variance Percentage. Divides schedule variance by budgeted cost to date. A negative value means the work is behind schedule.	SV÷BCWS

CV and SV calculations during the project will show you how the project is trending. If you want to see the result of those trends if they continue over the life of the project, you can do one more calculation:

Acronym	Variance	Calculation
EAC	Estimate at Completion. Recalculates the cost or completion date based on performance to date.	(Original Cost × ACWP) ÷ BCWP

Actual Cost for Work Performed (ACWP):
Actual Cost for Work Performed. The actual cost of the task so far.

Cost Variance (CV):
Difference between Budgeted Cost of Work Performed and Actual Cost of Work Performed.

Schedule Variance (SV):
Difference between Budgeted Cost of Work Performed and Budgeted Cost of Work Scheduled

Cost Variance Percentage (CVP):
Divides cost variance by budgeted cost. A negative value means a cost overrun.

Schedule Variance Percentage (SVP):
Divides schedule variance by budgeted cost to date. A negative value means the work is behind schedule.

Estimate at Completion (EAC):
Recalculates the cost or completion date based on performance to date.

TASK 8C-1

Doing Earned Value Analysis calculations

Objective: Doing Earned Value Analysis calculations

Setup: Your team has presented you with the following status data for the Develop Recipes work package: Actual work performed = 40%; actual cost to date = $2,500; budgeted cost for work package = $7,500; number of days scheduled = 30; # of days actual = 20.

1. In the table below, fill in the BCWS, BCWP, and ACWP for the Develop Recipes work package.

BCWS	
BCWP	
ACWP	

2. What is the cost variance for this work package? What does this number mean?

3. What is the schedule variance for this work package? What does this number mean? What calculation can you use to provide a more meaningful schedule variance number?

4. What is the cost variance for the work package? What is the cost variance percentage? What do these numbers mean?

Topic 8D

Getting Back on Track

When Do You Check for Variances?

In the heat of a project, it may be tempting to put off monitoring until a task is complete, until a work package is complete, or even until the entire project is complete. At that point, everyone will know exactly how the task, work package, or project performed against time and budget criteria. The flaw in the logic is that, after the fact, there is no longer time to fix problems and get the project back on track. By monitoring systematically, at frequent and predetermined time intervals, you will raise issues in time to deal with them.

A logical time to monitor is before each project status report is due. Stakeholders need to learn about variances, although different stakeholders may have a different need-to-know. Your project's reporting plan should spell out who to notify, and when.

Methodology for Dealing with Variances

When you discover project variances, what can you do to get the project back on track? It's important to face the issue and deal with it. Variances rarely correct themselves; in fact, they have a way of growing larger as early mistakes are perpetuated.

TASK 8D-1

Dealing with Variances

1. The first step in dealing with a variance is to find its cause. This may mean doing root cause analysis at the work package or even task level to find out what went wrong. For example, is a work package behind schedule because the software you ordered needs to be custom-installed on every computer? Is the task over budget because there weren't enough $10/hour people to do the work, so it had to be done by $15/hr people?

2. Next, plan to take corrective action. For example, can you install your software on a project server, rather than on each laptop? Can you borrow some $10/hr people from elsewhere in the project where there is some available float? Get creative, but consider the costs in time, money, and quality for each alternative. And be realistic. If the root problem is that a task was underestimated, re-estimate it now based on real-world knowledge, and determine its effect on the project as a whole.

3. Don't forget to determine overall project impact. Whatever the root cause identified above, try to identify other points in the project where similar problems may occur. For example, will you need to use the same software on another work package? Were you counting on a $10/hr labor pool for other tasks, too? If you have figured out a work-around for one work package, multiply its impact by the number of all the work packages where similar problems are likely to occur.

4. Finally, present the information to stakeholders. If the variances are beyond an acceptable level, get ready to negotiate trade-offs. Your original time/cost/quality criteria were based on certain assumptions. If the earlier assumptions were flawed, your stakeholders may have to change their success criteria. Whether this will mean adding budget, sliding the schedule out, or lowering the quality goal—or a mix of all three—depends on the project, your organization, and your industry.

Summary

During the Implementation Phase of the Project Management Life Cycle, the project manager must make sure that the team has what it needs to do its work, and smooth over any barriers that might get in the team's way. Monitoring performance is another key task. Project Managers can use simple variance identification or more complex Earned Value Analysis to track project performance. If the project gets off track and serious variances develop, the project manager works with stakeholders to negotiate the most expedient trade-offs of time, cost, and quality for the project.

Apply Your Knowledge 8-1

Suggested Time:
5 minutes

Objective: Use the status worksheet to collect simple variance information.

Instructions: Take a few moments to review this worksheet in your Project Portfolio. You will find a blank version on the CD-ROM that accompanies this book. The worksheet is meant to serve as a template. Use this status worksheet to collect simple variance information. You can use the information to create status charts, or to do an Earned Value Analysis.

Lesson Review

8A List three skills that a project manager needs to establish project momentum.

8B **What is the word for the difference between actual and estimated costs or time?**

8C **The benefit of conducting Earned Value Analysis is:**

_____ a. It provides a more accurate project baseline than other tracking methods.

_____ b. Management can understand Earned Value Analysis better than other measures.

_____ c. It allows you to see interrelationships between cost and schedule variances.

_____ d. It shows you how to get a project back on track.

8D **Why is it important to monitor for cost or schedule variances systematically?**

Project Reports

Data Files
L9AYK.doc

Lesson Time
20-30 minutes

Overview

"We're drowning in information and starving for knowledge."– Rutherford Rogers, New York Times, 1985

How can you keep your stakeholders up-to-date on project issues without drowning them in unnecessary information. Your communication plan should spell out what you will communicate and to whom. Your job will be to communicate clearly, succinctly, and systematically. The Status Report and the Change Request are two key reporting tools used by project managers.

Objectives

In order to discuss key elements of project management communications and reporting tools, you will:

9A **List and discuss elements of a project communications plan.**

Communications are critical to any project. How can the project manager keep stakeholders informed without overwhelming them with too much information? What information do team members need, and how will they access the information when they need it? These are some of the questions that a project communications plan should answer.

9B **List and discuss key elements of the project performance report and techniques for presenting performance-related information.**

Performance reporting is a key communications challenge for the project manager. This section outlines what should be included in a Project Performance Report and discusses methods for communicating complex performance-reporting information.

9C **Discuss when to issue a change request and what elements it should include.**

Changes to project scope or success criteria should be documented on a Project Change Request. This report documents when a change was made, the nature of the change, and who signed off on the change.

 # Topic 9A

Communications Overview

The Challenge of Project Communication

As you may have noticed, projects are information-rich environments. Stakeholders each playing different roles, need access to different levels of project information for decision making. Project managers must collect that information, archive it, and disseminate the right pieces of information to the right stakeholders at the right time, in a way that is clear, complete, but not overwhelming.

The Communications Plan

A communications plan helps the project manager and stakeholders to understand what information will be communicated, who is responsible for communicating it, when it will be communicated and updated, how it will be communicated, and how records will be kept. The communications plan should include:

- An outline of what documents will be collected, how they will be filed, and where they will be housed.

- A list of documents that will be published, outlining format and content areas, as well as the intended publication medium.

- A publication schedule for each document.

- A distribution list for each document.

- A policy statement on how to deal with corrections and updates to published documents.

TASK 9A-1

Creating a Communications Plan

1. Based on what you know about the Italian Cookbook project and project management in general, what documents should Frank Edwardson expect to publish during the Implementation Phase of the project? the Planning Phase?

Topic 9B

Project Performance Reports

Project Reports

Many project communications deal with performance reporting. Reports should answer these questions:

Type of Information	Key Questions
Status	Is the project on target? Are there problems or variances that need to be addressed?
Progress	What has the project team accomplished since the last update? Which work packages are complete, which partially complete, etc.
Project Forecast	Based on trends, what is the outlook for ongoing status and progress? Are there scope or goal changes that must be made in order to complete the project successfully?

STATUS:

PROJECT: PROGRESS:

PROS FORCAST:

Reporting Formats

As you learned in the last lesson, performance information can be complex. Part of your challenge is to convey that information in a way that stakeholders can grasp, in order to discuss the implications of the information. The table lists some communications formats that work particularly well for performance reporting.

Format	Uses
Gantt Chart 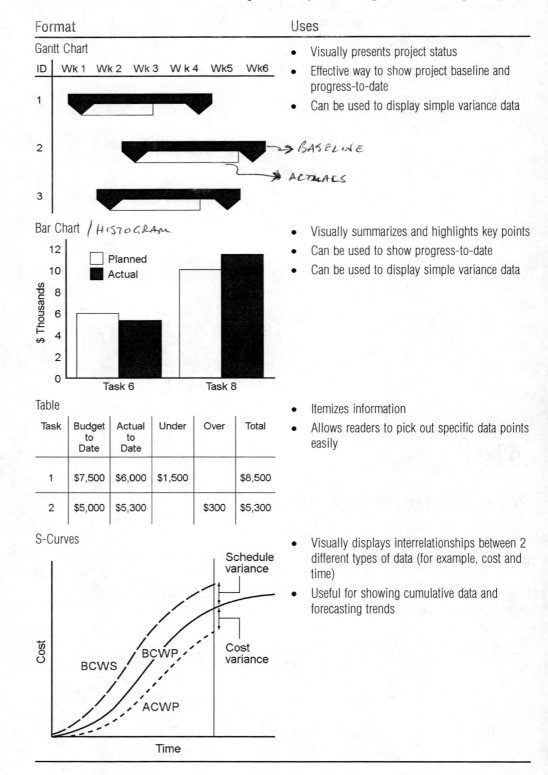	• Visually presents project status • Effective way to show project baseline and progress-to-date • Can be used to display simple variance data
Bar Chart / HISTOGRAM	• Visually summarizes and highlights key points • Can be used to show progress-to-date • Can be used to display simple variance data
Table	• Itemizes information • Allows readers to pick out specific data points easily
S-Curves	• Visually displays interrelationships between 2 different types of data (for example, cost and time) • Useful for showing cumulative data and forecasting trends

Did you notice that network logic diagrams were left off the list? For performance reporting, network logic diagrams tend to be overwhelmingly complex. Save them for working sessions with your project team. If you must use them with other stakeholders, create a summary Gantt Chart and use the network logic diagram to explode-out the detailed data.

TASK 9B-1

Selecting Reporting Formats

Objective: Identify the most appropriate reporting format for a given type of information.

1. **One of your work packages is going to run longer than expected. You need to update some of the functional managers from whom you have borrowed resources. What is a good way to display what you are doing and why?**

2. **Your Earned Value Analysis indicates that your project is running 5% over budget. By running an Estimate at Completion calculation, you find that it will likely overrun by 15% over the life of the project. What display format is most appropriate to show these trends?**

Topic 9C

Project Change Requests

Elements of a Change Request

Change happens, and on projects it happens a lot. Some changes may be initiated by you, while others may be initiated by other stakeholders. In either case, if the project scope or success goals for your project are changing, issue a *Project Change Request*. This report documents the reason for the change, the nature of the change, the timing of the change, and who signed off on the change.

Make your Change Request as specific as possible. It is important that everyone reading the document understands the exact nature of the change, and the implications of the change.

Project Change Request: documents details of project changes and who signed off on them.

A Change Request will help you solidify trade-off agreements and document sign-offs.

Change Requests can be formal documents, letters, memos, or even meeting minutes, depending on the preferences of the organization. Whatever the format, <u>be sure the Change Request includes:</u>

Element	Description
Change	Describe the change requested. Include specific criteria that can be used to measure the change.
Requested By	<u>Who</u> is requesting the change
Reason for Change	<u>Why</u> the change is being made; how the change will benefit the outcome of the project
Method of Change	<u>How</u> the change will be implemented.
Affected Parties	<u>Who will be affected</u> by the change
Affect on Success Criteria	<u>How</u> will the change affect: • Quality • Time • Cost
Backup Information	Any additional information that is needed to <u>support or explain the nature</u> of the change
Sign-Offs	<u>Who</u> approved the change
Date of Approval	<u>When</u> was the change approved

Summary

Communications are important in project management. A Communications Plan establishes the ground rules for what will be communicated, to whom, and when. It also establishes expectations for archiving and access to project information. Performance reporting is key aspect of project communications. Care should be taken to choose a reporting medium that will provide the necessary information without overwhelming the recipient. As a result of variance reporting or other situations, changes may be necessary to the project scope or objectives. A Change Request is used to document specific changes, the implications of the changes, and the parties signing off on the changes.

Apply Your Knowledge 9-1

Objective: Use the matrix to create a communications plan for your project

Instructions: Take a few moments to review this worksheet in your Project Portfolio. You will find a blank version on the CD-ROM that accompanies this book. The worksheet is meant to serve as a template. You can use it to help you set up and manage a communications plan for your project.

Handwritten margin notes:
— IMPACT OF NOT IMPLEMENTING THE CHANGE
— ALTERNATIVES TO NOT MAKING THE CHANGE

Lesson Review

9A List five types of information that should be covered in a communications plan?

9B Which type of display format is LEAST appropriate to conveying progress and status information to an executive team?

____ a. Network logic diagram

____ b. Data Table

____ c. Gantt Chart

____ d. S-Curve

9C What is the most important element of a change request?

Project Close-Out

Data Files
L10AYK.doc

Lesson Time
20-30 minutes

Overview

"Never embark on an enterprise unless you can see your way clear to the end of it." — Aesop

Do you remember the purpose of your project? Chances are, it was to create or improve some product, service, or process. Once your project output is complete, your role is to orchestrate the smoothest-possible hand-off, to shut down project operations, and to celebrate success before moving on to the next project.

Objectives

In order to discuss key activities of project close-out, you will:

10A   list major close-out activities.

What items should be on your project close-out punch list? This section discusses some of the activities you will want to include on your list.

10B   List and discuss elements to be included in project reports and evaluations.

What worked in a project and what did not? Who met expectations and who did not? As part of the Project Close-out, the project manager needs to consider lessons learned and evaluate project and personnel performance.

Topic 10A

Elements of Close-Out

The Project Close-Out Phase

Project Close-Out is the <u>final phase</u> of the project management life cycle—the time to hand over your project output to end users, close down operations, and get on with your life. Figure 10–1 shows the activities and milestone deliverables for this project phase.

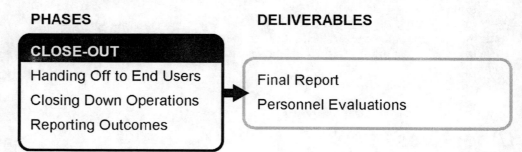

PHASES

CLOSE-OUT
Handing Off to End Users
Closing Down Operations
Reporting Outcomes

DELIVERABLES

Final Report
Personnel Evaluations

Figure 10-1: *Close-out phase of the project management life cycle.*

Project Hand-off

Handing off a project may sound simple, but it's actually a mini-project in its own right. Ideally, project hand-off should begin way back in the Initiation Phase of the project. The table below shows how hand-off positioning activities should be woven throughout the project management life cycle:

Main Project Activities	Hand-Off Activities
Define project stakeholders, scope, objectives.	• Define hand-off stakeholders, scope, objectives. • Share information with end-user stakeholders, and make sure they understand final project specifications. (This may include creating visuals or prototype models to help individuals visualize the project outcome) • Explain the project benefits, including the end-users' "what's in it for me" • Be ready to discuss any downsides for the end-users.
Plan main project schedule, costs, and resources.	• Plan hand-off schedule, costs, and resources. • Make sure end-user functional managers understand target hand-off dates and resource requirements • Work with end-users to plan *Change Management* initiatives • Make sure to include periodic end-user updates to your communications plan
Implement the work plan and monitor performance.	• Update end-user functional managers if target dates change • Implement Change Management initiatives so end-users are prepared for coming changes • Prepare individuals who will function as trainers or technical support during the initial hand-off
Close-Out project and hand-off to end-user functional managers	• Provide all deliverables as promised • Provide support to end-user functional managers through the hand-off period.

Change Management: Activities that help people accept and deal with changed circumstances or work processes.

As a project manager, keep in mind the importance of systematic communication in achieving a successful hand-off. Your project is all-important to you, but may seem unimportant to end-user functional managers. It is up to you to remind end-users of the project's purpose, target dates, and resource requirements—and perhaps to convince them of the project benefits, as well.

Other Close-Out Elements

Project hand-off is the glamorous side of the close-out phase—the moment when you see your project's output in the hands of end users. Other activities during the close-out phase center around managing an orderly ending to team activities. These elements include:

• Project close-out reporting

• Team personnel evaluations

• Shutting down project accounts

• Shutting down team operations

• Team celebration events

TASK 10A-1

Discussing Hand-Off Activities

1. Your publisher will begin to market the book as soon as you hand over the approved galleys. You have heard that the financial success of a book really depends on the buzz that is created with the publisher's sales reps—who then have to communicate that excitement to book dealers. When in the Project Management Life Cycle should you begin to work with the publisher to create buzz?

Topic 10B

Evaluation of People and Projects

Personnel Evaluation

Individuals on your project team spent a lot of time and energy on your project. Now it's time for them to move on—either back to their original positions, or to another assignment. They look to you, as project manager, to evaluate their performance and help their careers.

As project manager, you may be asked to write an entire performance evaluation, or contribute to another functional manager's evaluation of the employee's performance.

Once again, the evaluation process should have begun much earlier in the project, so the evaluation criteria you use for personnel evaluation should come as no surprise to anyone on the project. The table below shows personnel performance criteria should be created and communicated.

Main Project Activity	Evaluation Activity
Identify team members and create team charter	Identify behavior rules for team members
Plan work packages and identify resources	Identify measurable goals for each task; establish performance criteria for each task; assign tasks
Implement plan by performing work packages, reporting progress in team meetings, and monitoring overall project performance	Monitor task performance; provide feedback on performance as needed; provide feedback on team behavior as needed

TASK 10B-1

Discussing Personnel Evaluations

1. One of the assistant chefs on your Italian Cookbook team was a wonderful worker. She always showed up prepared, worked hard and smart, and was willing to do more than her share of project tasks. However, she often mentioned that she didn't see the point in attending project team meetings. In fact she skipped or was late for at least 50 percent of these required meetings. How should this affect her personnel evaluation?

The Final Report

By the end of a project, you will be a different person from the one who began the project. Some of your ideas will have succeeded; others will have failed. You may wish that you had done things differently, or that others had acted differently. Now, at the close-out of the project, is your time to sum up what you have learned on the project—and to help the organization learn how to do things better on the next project.

Your final project report should answer these questions:

- What happened in the project? What were the main milestones and activities?

- Who participated in the project? What did each person contribute to the project's completion?

- What was the project's final output? How did it measure up against the project's success criteria?

- What is the current status of the project's output? Is the hand-off complete or are there additional steps that must be handled by a hand-off team? Are there preliminary results that indicate acceptance by end users?

- Were mistakes made in the Initiation Phase that resulted in the need to rescope or redesign the project later? What were those mistakes? How could they be avoided next time?

- Were mistakes made in the Planning Phase that resulted in inaccurate estimates, inappropriate resource planning, or rework? What were the mistakes? How could they be avoided next time?

- Similarly, what mistakes were made in the Implementation and Close-Out Phases that should be avoided?

- What methods or ideas went well, and how might the organization re–use these in future projects?

- Do you have recommendations for new projects as a result of this project?

That's a lot of material to cover. Try to keep your report short, summarizing the written versions of "lessons learned" and "recommendations" parts. If possible, review these sections at greater length in a face-to-face meeting.

Keep the Final Report short. Provide detail about Lessons Learned and Recommendations in face-to-face meetings.

Summary

Project Close-Out activities include handing-off the project output, as well as closing down project activities, evaluating project personnel performance, and writing a final report. The seeds for the Close-Out activities were planted in the earlier phases of the Project Management Life Cycle, when hand-off plans and evaluation criteria were created. It's important to look back at the end of the project and learn from mistakes. These learnings should become "organizational learnings" that will provide guidance to project managers on future projects.

Apply Your Knowledge 10-1

Suggested Time:
5 minutes

Objective: Plan to develop your project management skills further.

Instructions: Take a few moments to review this worksheet in your Project Portfolio. You will find a blank version on the CD-ROM that accompanies this book. The worksheet is meant to serve as a template. You can use it to help you plan additional activities that may help you become a better project manager.

Lesson Review

10A Name four activities that take place during the Close-Out phase.

10B True or False? Criteria for personnel performance evaluation is set during the Close-Out Phase.

True or False? The final report should declare victory without commenting on problems or mistakes made during the project.

LESSON 1

Task 1A-1 Page 3

1. **Bob manages a group of tax return processors. Every day, his people interview clients, use the data to fill out tax returns, and compute the amount of tax owed. Is Bob's group assigned to a project or ongoing work? Why?**

Bob's group's work is ongoing work, because it is a repeating set of tasks, without a clear beginning or end point, producing essentially the same output each time.

Rita's team is developing a training manual to help new Tax Return Processors learn their jobs faster. Her team is made up of Tax Return Specialists, writers, and graphic designers who are assigned to the team part-time. Rita's work began when her manager gave her the assignment, and must be completed by January 1 in time for Human Resources to train the new Tax Return Processors who will be hired next year. Is Rita's team assigned to a project or ongoing work?

Rita's team's work is a project, because it is a one-time-only task, with a clear beginning and end point, producing a unique output (a training manual).

Who has the more difficult management job—Rita or Bob? Why?

Answers may vary, although all should agree that the two management jobs are difficult in different ways. For example, you might say that Rita's management job is more difficult because what she is trying to do has never been done before, or because she is dealing with a multi-disciplined team with conflicting priorities, or because her team also reports to other managers. Or, you might say that Bob's management job is more difficult because his group's work is more routine, so he must work harder to keep his group motivated.

Task 1B-1 Page 7

1. **In which project phase will the project's stakeholders set goals for the project?**

Project Initiation

2. **In which project phase will the scheduling and budgeting be done?**

Project Planning

3. **In which project phase does the project manager need to monitor whether work is progressing according to schedule and budget predictions?**

Project Implementation

4. **In which phase does the greatest expense typically occur? Why?**

Project Implementation, because the greatest amount of resources are dedicated to the project during that phase.

Task 1C-1 Page 9

1. **Standard chose Frank Edwards as project manager because they knew he had excellent communications skills. In what phases of the Italian Cookbook project will Frank need to use these skills? Will the communications be upwards, downwards, or sideways?**

Frank will need to use communications skills in all phases of the project. He will have to communicate upwards, reporting project status, answering stakeholder questions about deliverables, and negotiating for resources. He will have to communicate downwards, keeping team members informed about how they are progressing and what needs to be done to meet project goals. And he will have to communicate sideways, keeping Marketing and other functional managers updated so they are ready to handle the project after it is completed.

LESSON REVIEW 1

Topic 1-A

Which items below are characteristics of a project?

____ a. Only one person at a time is working on the task.

✓ b. The task has a clear beginning and ending.

____ c. The task results in the same output each time it is performed.

____ d. The resources required to perform the task are known based on previous experience.

Topic 1-B

The project phase in which budgets are created is commonly called the:

____ a. Initiation Phase.

✓ b. Planning Phase.

____ c. Implementation Phase.

____ d. Close-Out Phase.

Topic 1-C

List four skills needed by a project manager.

Answers should include any 4 of these: technical skills, planning skills, organizing skills, controlling skills, communications skills, leadership skills; motivation skills; team building skills; consensus building skills; conflict resolution skills; negotiation skills.

LESSON 2

Task 2A-1 Page 16

1. What success criterion is missing?

The expected quality level of the retooled line.

2. If you were Jennifer, what questions would you want answered?

Answers will vary, but here are a few:

- *What do you mean by "retooling?" What do you want the retooled line to be able to do that it can't do now?*
- *What are the quality expectations? For example, what productivity, cycle time, or defect goals must the new line be able to meet?)*
- *Are there other stakeholders besides the VP of Manufacturing? Is there general agreement on the success criteria?*
- *What company resources can be used?*
- *How will work get done during the retooling? Can the existing line be shut down completely during the retooling?*

Task 2B-1 Page 18

1. Does the napkin constitute a cost/benefit analysis? How useful are the figures provided on the napkin?

This is not a cost/benefit analysis. A cost-benefit analysis provides insights into budget parameters for the project. For example, if the cost-benefit analysis shows that the organization will benefit from a $500,000 project but that it will not recoup its investment on a $750,000 project, then the stakeholders may wish to define success criteria accordingly. In this case, there is a general guideline for the cost of book development, and you can get a sense for the potential profit if all goes perfectly. But there is no indication of what the minimum book profit has to be, which would tell Frank whether there is some negotiating room above $125,000. Also, there is no indication of the significance of that napkin! Who wrote it, and what did that person base the figures on?

2. What should the project manager do if inputs such as a feasibility study or cost/benefit analysis are not available for the project?

Answers will vary, depending on the circumstance. The project manager and stakeholders need to understand why a project was selected, what the strategic benefit to the organization is likely to be, and what cost constraints the project may be subjected to. In some organizations, this information is available only informally, but it is still adequate to the purpose. If the information is really unavailable, then the project manager should lead the stakeholders to define why the project was selected and what its strategic benefit is likely to be.

Task 2C-1 Page 20

2. Suppose that the project is in the Implementation Phase when Frank Edwardson learns that the Facilities Manager is refusing to make available the kitchen facilities that Frank was counting on. How can Frank use the Stakeholder Responsibility Matrix to help get what he needs?

Frank can refer to Stakeholder Responsibility Matrix whenever he needs to clarify roles and responsibilities or enforce a stakeholder commitment. In this example, if the resource commitment was documented in the Stakeholder Responsibility Matrix, Frank may want to ask the Project Sponsor to review this document with the Facilities Manager.

3. Frank has noticed that no customers were included on the stakeholder team! What should you do if you join a project late, and realize that a key stakeholder has been left out of the project definition activities?

It may be painful, but it is better to surface the stakeholder's requirements as early as possible. That way, the project success criteria can be renegotiated before the project goes further off course.

Task 2C-2 Page 21

1. What problem does the project solve?

Answers will vary, but might include: Problem is the erosion of sales and market share in Standard's existing market, and the lack of a product offering in the

2. What approach will be taken, for whom, and by when?

Answers will vary, but might include: Create a celebrity chef cookbook that will leverage Standard's reputation for health-conscious products, appeal to upscale food-lovers, and be available to booksellers by August 31.

3. During the Implementation Phase of the project, Frank Edwardson's team decides to develop a software program to automate the conversion between American and Italian measurement units. How can the Purpose Statement guide Frank and his team in deciding whether this activity is a good idea?

The Purpose Statement helps Frank stay on track and prevent being distracted by good ideas that don't really contribute to achieving the true purpose of the project. A good question to ask the team is, "Will this proposed activity actually help us achieve the project purpose?"

Task 2C-3 Page 23

1. What tasks does the project manager have to accomplish in the project? What output should result? What performance levels must be met?

Answers will vary, but may include:

- *Develop and test recipes (at least 100, must be accurate as verified by test, must meet low-fat criteria)*
- *Photograph 20 dishes (full-page color, look appealing)*
- *Layout text, photos, graphics (lots of white space; photos are page-sized)*
- *Identify and write anecdotal information and transitional text sections (anecdotes attributable to Mme. Tosca)*
- *Combine into book length galleys (not more than 200 pages, ready for production)*

Task 2C-4 Page 24

1. Which of these is out of scope for the Italian Cookbook project?

   ✓   a. A recipe for Fettucine Alfredo, Mme. Tosca's favorite Northern Italian pasta.

   ✓   b. The traditional breakfast food of Southern Italy.

   ____   c. Recipes for Southern Italian dishes that Mme. Tosca served at dinner parties she catered in the White House.

Task 2D-1 Page 26

1. **What should you do if you are asked to manage a project after the SOW is complete?**

   Review the SOW to make sure all elements are in place. If something is missing or unclear, work with the sponsor and stakeholders to thoroughly define project expectations before continuing on.

2. **What should you do if your company does not normally use a SOW in its projects, although the company does required all of the elements listed above?**

   Check with other project managers in your company to see how they handled the situation. It's possible that the SOW is called something else in your company. The document title doesn't matter—the point is to get all the elements in place and get a sign-off on them so you can move forward.

Task 2E-1 Page 27

1. **As project manager, Frank Edwardson will need to staff his project soon. How might he use the Project Charter for his staffing activities?**

   Answers will vary, but should include examples of using the Project Charter to prove to other managers that he is authorized to use resources. This may require hiring new personnel or requesting reassignment of existing personnel. Even with the Project Charter in hand, these requests may have to be negotiated carefully. Remember, project managers need to use good people skills throughout the project management life cycle!

LESSON REVIEW 2

Topic 2-A

What are the three basic success criteria for every project?

Time

Cost

Quality (customer satisfaction)

Topic 2-B

Which of these are activities that occur during the Initiation Phase of a project?

_____ a. Activity scheduling

_____ b. Conducting customer-satisfaction focus groups

✓ c. Defining time, cost, and quality criteria for the project

_____ d. All of the above are correct

Topic 2-C

List six items that define a project and explain the expectations for its success.

Stakeholder Responsibility Matrix; purpose statement; objectives statement; scope statement; review and sign-off plan; communications and reporting plan

Topic 2-D

Which of these elements should be included in a Statement of Work?

✓ a. Objectives

_____ b. Supplier Contracts

✓ c. Stakeholder Roles and Responsibilities

_____ d. Project Budget

Topic 2-E

What is the purpose of the Project Charter?

✓ a. Provides official authorization for the project

_____ b. States the project's success criteria

_____ c. Lists all team members assigned to the project

_____ d. Documents how the project team will report to stakeholders

LESSON 3

Task 3B-1 Page 37

5. **If you were the project manager for the Italian Cookbook project, how might you respond to the blank spaces?**

    Answers will vary, but should include the options of adding team members with the missing skills, or providing training for additional team members.

Task 3C-1 Page 38

1. **Can you think of an additional rule that might be included in the Meetings area?**

    Answers will vary. One example might require team members to turn off cell phones during meetings.

2. **Why do you think it is important to include items like "avoid blaming other team members" or "avoid making negative comments about other team members' ideas" in the rules?**

    Answers will vary, but should focus on the importance of building an atmosphere of trust and respect, so that people will not be afraid to offer creative ideas and solutions.

3. **Mme. Tosca is an invaluable asset to the team, but sometimes she can ramble on and waste too much time in meetings. You don't want to keep her from talking, but you want to make sure that you cover necessary topics and that other people get their opinions heard, too. How might you write a rule to address the Mme. Tosca problem (without hurting Mme. Tosca's feelings!)?**

    Answers will vary, but could include rules such as: keep comments short and to the point; limit comments to open–discussion time, and keep them to five minutes maximum; etc.

LESSON REVIEW 3

Topic 3-A

In which project phase should team building activities occur?

Team building begins in the initiation phase with activities directed specifically at the core project team. As the project progresses and implementation team members are added, additional team building activities should occur.

Topic 3-B

A Team Skills Matrix can be used to:

____ a. Break out skills needed for each project task.

____ b. Identify which team members have which skill sets.

____ c. Identify criteria that may be used to determine whether a team member has a particular skill set.

✓ d. All of the above.

Topic 3-C

List six areas that should be addressed on the Project Charter.

Meetings, record-keeping, behavior, decision making, resources, and communications.

Lesson 4

Task 4A-1 Page 43

1. What are some potential risks for this project?

Answers will vary, but here are a few possibilities: ability of the team to work together collaboratively; availability of Mme. Tosca to devote time to this project; availability of adequate kitchen facilities for cooking and testing recipes; potential conflicts with Mme. Tosca's existing TV sponsors;

Task 4A-2 Page 44

1. How would you categorize each answer in regard to probability and impact on the project?

Answers will vary.

Task 4A-3 Page 45

1. What type of risk management approach is this?

Transfer of risk

2. What type of risk management approach is this?

Avoidance of risk

3. What type of risk management approach is this?

Mitigation of risk

4. What type of risk management approach is this?

Acceptance of risk

LESSON REVIEW 4

Topic 4-A

List the four basic approaches to handling risk.

Acceptance, avoidance, transfer, mitigation

LESSON 5

Task 5A-1 Page 50

1. What is the sub-project in this example?

Final Draft

2. What are the summary tasks?

Incorporate revised recipes, incorporate revised photos, lay out pages; assemble; proofread

3. List some work packages that make up the summary task for "incorporate revised photos."

Answers may vary, but may include tasks such as: reshoot selected photos to incorporate authentic backgrounds; reprint selected photos to brighten colors; etc.

6. How might you use your completed WBS to assign task owners or identify resources needed?

Team can divide the work packages among themselves based on their functional specialty areas; functional specialists can then suggest resources that might be needed to complete the tasks.

7. How might you use the WBS in Risk Management planning?

Once the work packages have been broken down and assigned, the work package owner can conduct a risk management analysis for that work package.

Task 5B-1 Page 53

1. Assuming that we are diagramming tasks to show Finish-to-Start dependencies, what task must be completed before Task 5 begins?

Task 3.

2. What tasks could be done at the same time as Task 1? Must they be done at the same time as Task 1?

Task 6; it can be done anytime before task is complete.

3. An additional task, Task 7, has been added. It can't begin until Task 6 is completed. Task 5 is dependent on Task 7. Draw Task 7 where it belongs on Figure 5–3.

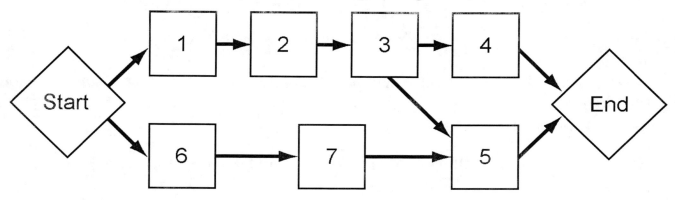

Figure 5.4: *Answer to Question #2*

LESSON REVIEW 5

Topic 5-A

Arrange these elements of a WBS into hierarchical order:

<u>3</u> Summary tasks

<u>2</u> Major sub-projects

<u>4</u> Work packages

<u>1</u> Project objective

Topic 5-B

Sequencing in which a task must be completed before the next task can begin is called

✓   a.   Start to Finish

____   b.   Start to Start

____   c.   Finish to Finish

____   d.   Finish to Start

Which tool lists summary activities, and then breaks them down into detailed activities or work packages?

Work Breakdown Structure

Which tool helps you visualize the dependency relationships among work packages?

Network logic diagram

LESSON 6

Task 6B-1 Page 60

2. What happens if Node 4 is delayed?

The project as a whole will be late, unless you offset the delay somewhere else on the critical path.

What happens if Node 3 is delayed?

There is some float time or allowable delay in Node 3, because it is not on the critical path. To learn how much float time is available, you must do the frontwards and backwards pass calculations.

3. Why does the earliest finish time have to be at 5 hours?

You are starting at hour 0, and your work will take 5 hours (duration time), so the earliest possible finish time is 5 hours. 0 + 5 = 5.

4. What is the earliest start time for Node 2? Why?

The earliest start time for Node 2 is 5, because Node 2 activities can begin as soon as Node 1 activities are finished.

5. What is the earliest finish time for Node 2? Why?

The earliest finish time for Node 2 is 9, because its tasks began at 5 hours and lasted for a 4 hour duration. 5 + 4 = 9.

6. The early start times for Nodes 3 and 4 are the same. Why?

Both Nodes can begin as soon as Node 2 is complete. Therefore, both Nodes begin at 9 hours.

7.   What are the early finish times for Nodes 3 and 4? Why?

Node 3's early finish is 15, because it had a 6–hour duration; Node 4's early finish is 19, because it had a 10–hour duration.

9.   Complete the forward pass calculation for the other nodes.

Node 6's early start is 24; early finish is 34. Node 7's early start is 24; early finish is 34. Node 8's early start is 24; early finish is 32. Node 9's early start is 34; early finish is 54.

12. What are the Late Start and Late Finish amounts for Nodes 6, 7, and 8?

All three nodes have a Late Finish of 34 (carried backward from node 9). Node 6 and Node 7 both have a Late Start of 24, because they both have a duration of 10 (34 — 10 = 24). Node 8 has a Late Start of 26 (34 — 8 = 26).

13. Now you have a problem. What should the Late Finish of Node 5 be, and why?

The LF of Node 5 is 24. Logically, if you assigned a Late Finish of Node 5 as 26, then you would be starting Nodes 6 and 7 before you completed Node 5. In a backwards pass, when an activity is followed by 2 or more activities with different LSs, always adopt the lowest value for the preceding node's LF.

14. What are the LS and LF amounts for all other nodes on the diagram?

Node 3: LS = 13; LF = 19. Node 4: LS = 9; LF = 19. Node 2: LS = 5; LF = 9. Node 1: LS = 0; LF = 5.

16. Once you identify float, what can you do with this information?

Answers will vary, but should focus on the idea that project managers can use this time to manage resources on the project. For example, if there is float time in Node 3, perhaps some of those resources can be reassigned temporarily to Node 4 to get that work done more quickly.

LESSON REVIEW 6

Topic 6-A

Why should the project team participate in the scheduling process?

____ a. Team participation is likely to make the scheduling process go faster.

✓ b. Team participation allows individuals who are closer to the actual tasks to be responsible for estimating the duration of the task.

✓ c. Individuals are more likely to commit to meeting a deadline if they participated in setting it.

Topic 6-B

In order to calculate the critical path, in what order must you do these activities?

2   Perform forwards and backwards pass calculations

3   Identify activities with float

1   Assign duration estimates to each node on the network logic diagram

LESSON 7

Task 7A-1 Page 69

1. **Give a specific example of each cost category and explain how you would compute it. (Example: Labor: Assistant chefs (2) × # hours and overtime hours in each work package**

Answers will vary. Here is one example for each category:

- *Labor: Assistant chefs (2) × # of hours and overtime hours in each work package*
- *Facilities: Kitchen rental × 6 months*
- *Equipment: Stockpot (6) × purchase price*
- *Supplies: printer paper (24 reams) × purchase price*
- *Special Expenses: Food stylist × contract price*

Task 7B-1 Page 70

2. In the Test Recipes work package, you expect to need an assistant chef for 10 weeks. You expect that the assistant chef will work 10 hours a day, from Monday to Friday. An assistant chef's hourly rate is $20/hr for an 8–hour day. Standard Publishing's overtime rate is time-and-a-half. Calculate the total labor cost estimate for the assistant chef's work in this work package.

    Labor Class: Assistant Chef; Hourly Rate (Regular): $20/hr; # of regular hours, 400; Reg Hours Cost, $8,000; Overtime Rate (1.5×): $30/hr; # of overtime hours: 100; Overtime Hours Cost, $3,000; Total Cost: $11,000.

3. In the Photograph Recipes work package, you expect to need a professional photographer on a one-day-a-week basis, from 9 to 5, for 4 weeks. A professional photographer's hourly rate is $50/hr for an 8 hour day. What is the total labor estimate for the photographer?

    $2,000 ($400 per day × 5 days).

Task 7C-1 Page 72

2. You need to reduce the labor cost for work package #2. Do you see a way to eliminate some of the cost? How might your strategy affect cost, time, and quality?

    Answers will vary. You can cut some cost by eliminating the overtime. You can do this by lengthening the schedule (affects time to complete the project, assuming this work package is on critical path), or by hiring an additional staffer to take over some of the work (may add overhead cost, may result in using more of the senior chef's time to manage two assistants, may cause inconsistencies in quality).

3. You need to shorten the work schedule. You are considering hiring two photographers, and reducing the task time for each one to 20 hours. What tools might you use when you make this decision? What is the likely impact on time, cost, and quality?

    Creating a network logic diagram for the work package will help you determine its internal dependencies. If the food stylist will complete all of the food preparation and hand over all of the food to be photographed at the same time, then the two–photographer idea might work. If the food stylist is preparing one dish at a time for photography, all that you will accomplish is having two photographers sitting around waiting for the food stylist. By splitting the job, you may incur extra cost for equipment and supplies, you may need extra facilities for shooting and developing photos, you may create an element of inconsistency that can affect quality, and you create a more difficult management challenge for the work package manager.

LESSON REVIEW 7

Topic 7-A

What cost category is usually the biggest cost component in a project budget?

Labor costs.

Topic 7-B

Which of these items is a true statement?

____ a. Labor rate multiplies hourly rate times regular hours, but should not include overtime.

____ b. The hourly rate should be the same for all workers in a given work package.

__✓__ c. Labor estimates typically include labor costs for team members whose salaries are already being paid by other departments.

Topic 7-C

You need to reduce your labor cost estimates by 10%. You know that your projected overtime costs account to 10% of the labor estimate. Name three factors you should examine before deciding to cut out the overtime.

Answers will vary, but should include: cost of the project (i.e. are there other costs that will accrue as a result of reducing the overtime?); time to complete the project (i.e. is overtime on the critical path, or does it represent float time?); quality of the project output (i.e. will we be able to produce a product that meets our quality criteria if we don't work the extra hours?)

LESSON 8

Task 8A-1 Page 77

1. **From your organization, what is an example of a boundary management task that a project manager might be expected to perform?**

Answers will vary. One possible example: arrange for special payment terms for a crucial piece of equipment that must be delivered just-in-time. In such a case, boundary management may include negotiating directly with a functional manager, or working indirectly through the project sponsor.

Task 8B-1 Page 79

1. **Based on the baseline chart, what is the schedule status of Work Package #2?**

Work Package #2 appears to be ahead of schedule by about 1 week.

2. **Based on the variance bar chart, what is the status of Task #4?**

It appears to be over budget by about 50 percent.

Task 8C-1 Page 84

1. In the table below, fill in the BCWS, BCWP, and ACWP for the Develop Recipes work package.

BCWS	
BCWP	
ACWP	

BCWS = 5,000 (20/30 × $7500); BCWP = 3,000 (40% x 7500); ACWP = 2,500

2. What is the cost variance for this work package? What does this number mean?

3,000 - 2,500 = 500; the work package is under budget by $500 so far.

3. What is the schedule variance for this work package? What does this number mean? What calculation can you use to provide a more meaningful schedule variance number?

3,000 - 5,000 = -2000; the work package is behind schedule by $2000 worth of work; by calculating SVP (schedule variance percentage), you can translate schedule variance into a percentage of the overall schedule for the work package (SV% = -40%, or 40% behind schedule.)

4. What is the cost variance for the work package? What is the cost variance percentage? What do these numbers mean?

CV = 3000 - 2,500; CVP = .16, or 16%; in other words, the work package is 16% under budget.

Lesson Review 8

Topic 8-A

List three skills that a project manager needs to establish project momentum.

Answers may vary, but may include: boundary management, team building, conflict management, upwards and downwards communication.

Topic 8-B

What is the word for the difference between actual and estimated costs or time?

Variance

Topic 8-C

The benefit of conducting Earned Value Analysis is:

_____ a. It provides a more accurate project baseline than other tracking methods.

_____ b. Management can understand Earned Value Analysis better than other measures.

✓ c. It allows you to see interrelationships between cost and schedule variances.

_____ d. It shows you how to get a project back on track.

Topic 8-D

Why is it important to monitor for cost or schedule variances systematically?

By systematically monitoring project performance, you can spot deviations that might threaten the project while there is still time to correct problems and remedy the situation.

LESSON 9

Task 9A-1 Page 91

1. **Based on what you know about the Italian Cookbook project and project management in general, what documents should Frank Edwardson expect to publish during the Implementation Phase of the project? the Planning Phase?**

Answers will vary, but might include these ideas. During the Implementation Phase, Frank will probably concentrate on publishing summary versions of the Statement of Work, and distributing them to stakeholders and potential core team members. His communications goals during this phase are limited to creating visibility for the project and himself as project manager. During the Planning Phase, his communications goals are to establish credibility for the project plan, get stakeholders to buy-in to the plan and begin to commit resources to it, document any decisions that have been made, and to generally create a sense of momentum around the project. His publications, therefore, might include newsletters that familiarize stakeholders with the credentials of team members, memos that keep stakeholders abreast of planning activities, as well as meeting agendas and minutes. Of course, at the end of the Planning Phase, he will submit planning deliverables and get sign off on them. During the Implementation Phase, his communications goals must expand along with his distribution list: He needs to keep team members aware of one another's progress; he needs to maintain the enthusiasm and interest of stakeholders; he needs to keep functional managers aware of upcoming events that may require the use of their resources; and he must keep the stakeholders aware of project performance and variance situations. He might use a combination of progress or status reports, meeting agendas; team meeting minutes; newsletters, personal memos and reminders, and formal performance reports to the stakeholders.

Task 9B-1 Page 93

1. **One of your work packages is going to run longer than expected. You need to update some of the functional managers from whom you have borrowed resources. What is a good way to display what you are doing and why?**

   Answers may vary, but a Gantt Chart showing baseline and actual schedules may be your best bet.

2. **Your Earned Value Analysis indicates that your project is running 5% over budget. By running an Estimate at Completion calculation, you find that it will likely overrun by 15% over the life of the project. What display format is most appropriate to show these trends?**

   Answers may vary, but should include: S-curves to show cumulative trends, possibly backed up by tables of data for in-depth discussion of problems.

LESSON REVIEW 9

Topic 9-A

List five types of information that should be covered in a communications plan?

- *An outline of what documents will be collected, how they will be filed, and where they will be housed*
- *A list of documents that will be published, outlining format and content areas, as well as the intended publication medium*
- *A publication schedule for each document*
- *A distribution list for each document*
- *A policy statement on how to deal with corrections and updates to published documents*

Topic 9-B

Which type of display format is LEAST appropriate to conveying progress and status information to an executive team?

✓ a. Network logic diagram

___ b. Data Table

___ c. Gantt Chart

___ d. S-Curve

Topic 9-C

What is the most important element of a change request?

A specific description of the nature of the change that is requested.

LESSON 10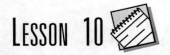

Task 10A-1 Page 100

1. **Your publisher will begin to market the book as soon as you hand over the approved galleys. You have heard that the financial success of a book really depends on the buzz that is created with the publisher's sales reps—who then have to communicate that excitement to book dealers. When in the Project Management Life Cycle should you begin to work with the publisher to create buzz?**

   Answers will vary, but should reflect the idea that hand-off begins well before the close-out phase. For example, during the initiation phase, you should identify sales/marketing stakeholders and find out what makes a book worthy of buzz. In the planning phase, you might want to plan some marketing-related milestones that would relate to buzz—for example, maybe you should plan to invite sales reps to some of your recipe-testing activities, or maybe you should create a tasting-buffet hand-off event for sales reps. During the implementation phase, you would carry out your plans work at communicating with the sales/marketing stakeholders and sales reps and keep them updated on your plans. During the close-out phase, carry out any hand-off plans.

Task 10B-1 Page 101

1. **One of the assistant chefs on your Italian Cookbook team was a wonderful worker. She always showed up prepared, worked hard and smart, and was willing to do more than her share of project tasks. However, she often mentioned that she didn't see the point in attending project team meetings. In fact she skipped or was late for at least 50 percent of these required meetings. How should this affect her personnel evaluation?**

   Answers will vary, but should reflect the fact that team behavior represented a portion of the performance criteria for the job. Clearly, the assistant chef's unwillingness to participate in team meetings made things more difficult for others on the team. She made group decision-making harder, she made team communication more complex, and her absence was probably a morale-buster. Her performance evaluation should reflect those facts.

LESSON REVIEW 10

Topic 10-A

Name four activities that take place during the Close-Out phase.

Answers should include four of these: hand-off to end users, close-out reporting, performance evaluation, shut-down of project activities, team celebration events

Topic 10-B

True or False? Criteria for personnel performance evaluation is set during the Close-Out Phase.

False.

True or False? The final report should declare victory without commenting on problems or mistakes made during the project.

False. It's important for the organization to learn from the mistakes, as well as to reap the benefits of the project's success.

Actual Cost for Work Performed (ACWP)
Actual Cost for Work Performed. The actual cost of the task so far.

Backwards Pass
Calculating the Late Start and Late Finish times for project work

Budgeted Cost for Work Performed (BCWP)
Also known as Earned Value. The percentage of the task budget that corresponds to the tasks's completion status.

Budgeted Cost for Work Scheduled (BCWS)
Budgeted Cost for Work Scheduled. (The amount you budgeted for a task between its start date and today.

core team
Key individuals who represent the major activities that the team will undertake during the project.

Cost Variance (CV)
Difference between Budgeted Cost of Work Performed and Actual Cost of Work Performed.

Cost Variance Percentage (CVP)
Divides cost variance by budgeted cost. A negative value means a cost overrun.

Critical Path
Network path with the longest total duration. Items on the critical path cannot be delayed or the project as a whole will be late.

Deliverable
An output from a project management activity. Deliverables from each phase are used to manage the next phases of the project.

dependencies
Relationships among work packages that determine the sequence in which work should be performed.

discretionary dependency
a dependency relationship which is imposed due to organizational preference or other optional criterion.

Earned Value Analysis
A method for monitoring project progress which measures both time and cost performance.

Earned Value
Also known as Budgeted Cost for Work Performed. The percentage of the task budget that corresponds to the tasks's completion status.

external dependency
a dependency relationship which arises from activities outside of your project, and possibly even outside of your organization.

boundary management
Managing the interfaces between your functional or project area, and those outside it.

Change Management
Activities that help people accept and deal with changed circumstances or work processes.

duration of effort
The total time needed to complete a task, including waiting times.

Estimate at Completion (EAC)
Recalculates the cost or completion date based on performance to date.

Float
Extra time available to do a task

Forward Pass
Calculating the Early Start and Early Finish times for project work

GLOSSARY

Impact of risk
Degree of seriousness of the risk's consequences.

implementation team
Project team members who help to carry out activities planned by the Core Team.

Initiation Phase
The project phase in which project mission, goals, and scope are defined. The output of the Initiation Phase is a Statement of Work.

mandatory dependency
a dependency relationship in which there is only one logical sequence of activities.

Network Logic Diagram
A scheduling tool that displays the interrelationships among project work packages.

Probability of risk
Likelihood that a problem will occur

Project Baseline
A snapshot of your original schedule and budget plans.

project budget
A plan for how you will spend money on each work package in a project.

Project Change Request
documents details of project changes and who signed off on them.

Project Gate
The end point of a project phase; a formal review time at which stakeholders make a go/no-go decision about continuing the project. Also known as Project Milestone.

Project Goals
How you intend to accomplish your project purpose, and what success criteria you intend to meet. Often referred to as project goals and objectives.

Project management
The planning, organizing, staffing, scheduling, leading, and controlling of work activities to achieve a pre-defined outcome on time and within budget.

Project Milestone
The end point of a project phase; a formal review time at which stakeholders make a go/no-go decision about continuing the project. Also known as Project Gate.

Project Objectives
How you intend to accomplish your project purpose, and what success criteria you intend to meet. Often referred to as project goals and objectives.

project scope
What is and is not included in your project.

project team
Individuals who collectively possess the skills to do a project, and who are committed to working together to reach the project goals.

Project
Work that has a specified beginning and ending and that produces a unique output.

Risk
Uncertainty. Things that can go wrong and negatively impact the cost, time, or quality of a project.

Schedule Variance (SV)
Difference between Budgeted Cost of Work Performed and Budgeted Cost of Work Scheduled

Schedule Variance Percentage (SVP)
Divides schedule variance by budgeted cost to date. A negative value means the work is behind schedule.

scope creep
Additional task items that are added to the project and that make it difficult to achieve project goals.

SOW
Statement of Work. It describes the work that will be performed in the project.

Stakeholder
Someone who has a business interest in the outcome of the project. Although most stakeholders are project team members, they are not required to be. For example, senior managers or customers may be key stakeholders, but do not personally participate in project work.

Statement of Work
Describes the work that will be performed in the project.

Status Data
The current completion level of your project.

task time
The amount of labor or resource time it will take to complete the activities in a task.

Variance
Difference between planned and actual status

Work Breakdown Structure (WBS)
Chart breaking down milestones and tasks that must be accomplished in a project.

Work Packages
Detailed tasks and/or sub-tasks that can be used in assigning, estimating, scheduling, and controlling project work.

Work Packages
Detailed tasks that must be performed in a project. The Work Package should include a statement of performance criteria.

INDEX